# Everything You Always Wanted to Know About HEAVEN But Didn't Know Where to Ask

JEANNE REJAUNIER

Copyright © 2014 Jeanne Rejaunier
All rights reserved.
ISBN:10-1500506591
ISBN-13-978-1500506599

## DEDICATION

To the eternal lives of Mary Weddell, Miriam Willis, Glenn Dies, Violet Stevens, Connie Smith, Tasma Carey, Margaret Branchflower, Miriam Albplanalp, Esther Barnes, Esther and Bill Estabrook, Gertrude and Linda Clark, George Flournoy, Christine Adler (aka Carmen Austin), Sylvia and Andrew Howe, Elizabeth Kirby, Ruth Thomas, Ruth and Frank Crandell, Rowena and Ralph Meeks; the Stones: Barbara, Willard and Jennifer Stone; Diana Davis, Jack Spahr, Katie and John #1; Grace Hale, Yvonne (Vonnie) and John Branchflower; the Cope family: Dale, Mary Jean, Beth, and John Cope; Lola Grube, Patti, Emily, Alma Johnson, Lenore, Ruby, Frances, Doris, Henriette Koerselman, Sandra, Helen and Ed von Gehr, Helen Marsh, Helen Flatwed, Helen DeCamp, Bernard Burry, Ellen King, Shelley O'Day, Eve Bruce, Judith Porter, Evelyn Swanson, Mary Werti, the three Virginias, Louise Eggleston, Elizabeth, Eva Totah, Marilyn, Jane, Rosemary, Kathy, Woodie, Avis, Lorna Lane, Hank, Gene Haffner, Fred Adler, Joanne, Lu Ann Horstman, June, Frieda, Lois, Dorothy, Bill and Clara Jackson, and everyone else I may have missed who shared the beautiful evenings in Pasadena and nighttimes in the Planes of Heaven - some with us still, others now living on the Other Side, all knowing there is one world without end, Amen.

# CONTENTS

Dedication
Acknowledgments
Preface
Introduction
Chapter One – Snapshots: The First Ten Planes of Heaven
Map/Chart I – The Subplane/1st Plateau of Heaven
Points of Interest on the 1st Plateau/Subplane of Heaven
Chapter Two - Picturing Reality Beyond Earth
Chapter Three – From the Shadow World to the Real World – Alive in the Afterlife
Chapter Four – The Other Face of the Afterlife
Chapter Five - The War and Accident Arena
Chapter Six - Visitations and Co-Minglings Between Heaven and Earth
Chapter Seven - The Invisibles – Power Stations, Bands, Hierarchies, Angels
Chapter Eight – BabyLand and Children's Land
Chapter Nine - How Mary Received Enlightened Teachings
Chapter Ten - Nights in the Heavenlies – Travel, Teaching, Tests
Chapter Eleven– Recalls and Questions
Chapter Twelve – Color, the Channel and Keynotes
Chapter Thirteen - Mary Answers Class Questions
Chapter Fourteen– Prelude to the 1st and 2nd Planes of Heaven
Map/Chart II – The 1st and 2nd Planes of Heaven
Points of Interest on the 1st and 2nd Planes of Heaven
Chapter Fifteen - The 1st Plane of Heaven
Chapter Sixteen – The 2nd Plane of Heaven
Chapter Seventeen– The Mount of Renunication
Chapter Eighteen – The Animal Kingdom and More Class Questions
About the Author
Three Chapters from Jeanne Rejaunier's *Planes of the Heavenworld*
Other Books by Jeanne Rejaunier
Critics' Reviews - *The Beauty Trap*
Coming Soon from Jeanne Rejaunier
How to Contact Jeanne Rejaunier

## ACKNOWLEDGMENTS

My deepest gratitude to Elizabeth Kirby, without whose invaluable help this book could not have been written. Elizabeth and Fred Kirby lovingly oversee the website http://creativecolor.org, which has done such an admirable job keeping alive the teachings of Mary Dies Weddell.

What a blessing that Mary Weddell, Miriam Willis and Jack Spahr created the unique and invaluable maps/charts of the 1st Plateau/Subplane, and the 1st and 2nd Planes of Heaven pictured in this book.

Thanks so much to Geoffrey Wynkoop, my wonderful Facebook friend, for his expertise in restoring the maps/charts from their degraded state to perfection.

Thanks to my son Vadim Newquist for his much appreciated cover design, and to Sylvia Howe for the beautiful portrait she painted of my poodle Gordy and me in front of the Temple of Wisdom, which decorates the back cover.

Thanks to Mary's granddaughter, Sheila Smith, and to all those others who collaborated on the book *Creative Color Analysis*, especially the late Miriam Willis, who was so dear to all of us; the late Margaret Branchflower, Esther Barnes, and Miriam Albplanalp.

And of course, tremendous thanks to Mary Weddell. Words cannot begin to express my gratitude for her presence and many decades of guidance in my life – here and hereafter.

# PREFACE

The literary genre of life after death, Heaven and the Afterlife is a popular one today. Everybody wants to know what awaits us after we leave this world. Most books on the subject are based either on near death experiences (NDE), mediums' channeling guides and discarnates from the Other Side, automatic writing, past life regressions, or information conveyed by subjects under hypnosis.

**EVERYTHING YOU ALWAYS WANTED TO KNOW ABOUT HEAVEN But Didn't Know Where to Ask** falls into a groundbreaking new category. It derives from my own and others' personal experiences as a group of 60 or more people of similar mind, who, over a period of decades, met during weekly Friday evenings in Pasadena, California, under the guidance of mentor and master teacher Mary Dies Weddell, whose extensive knowledge of ancient languages, esoteric truth and inspired teachings influenced thousands in America and abroad. While many of the elements mentioned in other titles on Heaven and the Afterlife are corroborated, with Mary's help and that of her exceptional senior teacher Miriam B. Willis, our class ventured into areas unexplored in previously published works.

Mary Dies Weddell (1886-1980), was a remarkable woman who became my spiritual "guru" in 1966, whose teachings I have followed for nearly half a century on both sides of life. Seer, musician (piano, organ, voice); author of four books; specialist in Egyptology and hieroglyphics; linguist, particularly in Sanskrit, ancient Hebrew, Aramaic, and Greek, Mary was one of the translators of the Dead Sea Scrolls. The underlying theme of all Mary's work is self knowledge leading to self mastery. Through two peerless, unique original courses, "Creative Color Analysis" and "The Planes of Heaven," Mary enabled us, her students, to see more deeply into ourselves and to understand more fully the awe inspiring structure and purpose of creation here and hereafter.

My first book about the other side of life, **PLANES OF THE HEAVENWORLD**, was based on personal recollections of Mary's classes, plus a few hundred pages of my difficult to read pencil and double sided leaky ball point pen notes. Soon after publication, I was contacted by class member Elizabeth Kirby, offering to share several thousand pages of typed transcripts which she had inherited from class members who had died. These I scanned and converted to word processing format. Culled and edited from some 6000 pages of transcripts, **EVERYTHING YOU EVER WANTED TO KNOW ABOUT HEAVEN But Didn't Know Where To Ask** focuses on the 1$^{st}$ Plateau/ Subplane and the 1$^{st}$ and 2$^{nd}$ Planes of Heaven.

Of enormous help to us as Mary's students was a series of maps/charts of Heaven we were provided that cite hundreds of heavenly points of interest, the descriptions and functions of which were elaborated on in class. The first two of these maps, naming more than one hundred locations of Heaven, their purposes and how they pertain to man's growth and ongoing in both worlds, are included in this book, namely: the 1$^{st}$ Plateau/Subplane (Map/Chart I), and the 1$^{st}$ and 2$^{nd}$ Planes (Map/Chart II). These two maps should provide a helpful guide to readers interested in learning about important preliminary regions of the invisible world. A projected six or more books in the series, which will explore Heaven's 3$^{rd}$ through 10$^{th}$ Planes, will include appropriately matching maps/charts as well. Mary's classes sometimes included a question and answer segment, a format which I have adapted freely in this book.

Life and death are one coexistent reality. When the silver cord is severed in "death," and we depart this world, crossing over to the other side of life to inhabit another dimension of reality, our consciousness goes along with us to the extent that we have developed it here on Earth. It is a sign of wisdom to give thought to the next life and to seek mastery in both worlds. Mary's revelations of "Color and the Channel" (Chapter 12) and "night work" in the temples of Heaven (Chapter 10) increase our development and enrich our lives significantly. Chapters 3-8 and 14-17 describe activities that occur in specific areas of the Heaven World, both for discarnates who inhabit those regions, and for us on Earth who as seekers travel there nightly in our spiritual consciousness to enhance our lives here and beyond.

As Mary's students, we were so fortunate to have a highly evolved, devoted and loving teacher endowed with the ability to take her students "out" at night to visit the many vast and awesome areas of Heaven. Readers without such an Earth teacher may wonder how they can do likewise. The good news is all seekers who so desire can be taken out by a heavenly teacher to develop their souls, prepare for the next life, and reap rewards both in the here and now and in the Afterlife. How this may be realized is but one of the numerous subjects covered in **EVERYTHING YOU ALWAYS WANTED TO KNOW ABOUT HEAVEN But Didn't Know Where To Ask.**

# INTRODUCTION

Since the beginning of time, as far back as man has been able to travel in consciousness, it has been the plan, always, for a priest, a teacher, a guru, someone who had knowledge of the spirit world, to take a small group with them to the Other Side. Having mastered laws governing the ascent and descent of the soul between Heaven and Earth, one of Mary Weddell's special gifts was the ability to take students over at night to the invisible realms for spiritual training. Over a period of many years in our night work, our class visited hundreds of temples and other areas of the Heaven World and brought back recollections that made a difference in our lives. What an array of subjects we touched on. Some, raised in this book, include:

What transpires after death: the procedure and protocol for every soul that arrives via the River of Life to the Landing Field on the 1$^{st}$ Plateau of Heaven in the Afterlife, and what happens after that; the netherworld, (Purgatory, Hell, the Magnetic Field); the Suicide Plane; war and accident victims; the Pattern World; music and art in Heaven; the invisibles: angels, teachers, guides and hierarchies; power stations; Babyland, Children's Land, the Animal Kingdom; clearing the subconscious to advance spiritually; dreams and visions; testing; our plan of life; earning our future station; communication between Heaven and Earth; visiting our departed loved ones on the Other Side, living in eternity now ... and more.

We are part of the divine plan of spiritual growth through the Planes of Heaven, both here and hereafter. The plane we earn from development in our Earth life will become our home in the Afterlife. As Mary asked, if you're planning a trip, wouldn't you want to know something about the place you're going? Now, while we're living here, is the time to become acquainted with that invisible land all of us will someday inhabit, and strengthen ties with the life beyond to which we are eternally linked.

Life is a gift, and what we do with it counts. It is truly one world without end, amen.

# CHAPTER ONE
# SNAPSHOTS: THE FIRST TEN PLANES OF HEAVEN

This book covers the **1st Plateau/Subplane**, and the **1st** and **2nd Planes** of Heaven. Future books in the series will delve into the **3rd** through the **10th Planes**.

A brief summary of the first ten Planes of Heaven follows:

The slowest vibrating dimension beyond the Earth plane is what Mary called the **1st Plateau/Subplane**. It is to this Plateau that the soul first goes at the transition of death, where we begin consciousness of our whereabouts, reckoning with who we are and what we can do with life in the Afterlife. The Subplane/1st Plateau caters to the recently deceased's recovery, orientation and decisions. The slowest vibrational level of the 1st Plateau/ Subplane is the Magnetic Field, which some teachings call the Astral World, where those souls who are earthbound dwell following death. The Magnetic Field partakes very strongly of the material or magnetic conditions which bound it. Sections of the Plateau/Subplane also contain undesirable areas such as Hades (Hell) and Purgatory, as mentioned in numerous religious and philosophical teachings.

The **1st Plane** interpenetrates the Earth at its center and extends out far beyond the surface of the physical Earth. The outer surface of the 1st Plane upon which its inhabitants dwell is many leagues out in space beyond the surface of the Earth. This plane is instinctive, instructive and expressive; it is a plane of adjustment and expansion, the plane of examination, also known as the plane of development. Here, we are confronted by certain questions: What is our degree of spiritual development? How many fundamental issues of spirit have we absorbed? How much do we practice spiritual principles? Do I really know myself? Do I know my purpose in life?

The **2nd Plane** is the Afterlife home of discarnate secularists, atheists, agnostics, materialists and unbelievers. It is a moral plane; that is, we face moral issues and make decisions to do things over again. Important parts of this plane are five principles in five temples that begin with

"Re:" Revelation, Remembrance, Retribution, Renunciation, and Redemption. (In Greek, re means going into, as to contemplate). On the 2nd Plane, one is in an area of instruction, designed to provide for the neglects and failures of life.

The **3rd Plane**: Everyone has a home on this plane, although there are also homes on every plane. Faith in God is strong here. A plane of homes, religion and places of worship, the 3rd Plane fosters the importance of the Sabbath carried over into everyday life. Those on this plane can be awakened and go on to the Halls of Learning.

The **4th Plane** is the citadel of fourth dimensional thinking, cosmic consciousness, and self mastery. This is also called the Prayer Plane. We are reminded that our desires and intents are so often impulses without forethought. Our need is to know and follow the prompting of spirit within. Here one becomes receptive for service by higher teachers.

The **5th Plane** is where dreams and visions are revealed to the awakened soul. Spiritual sensing quickens as does creative thinking. The test of faith here is how much of nonessentials have I relinquished? Our greatest tests before one of the heavenly hierarchies include answering the questions: who am I, and why am I here.

The **6th Plane** is a pivotal plane — the mystic gate where we learn to balance our spiritual and physical bodies. Adopting new relationships and armed by metamorphosis, we are learning of the law governing ascent and descent of soul between Heaven and Earth, enabling us to visit Earth alone, without a higher teacher, and look in on our loved ones still living on Earth.

The **7th Plane** is where all previous tests are repeated in preparation for the 8th Plane. It is a plane of divine imagination, perseverance, and desire to share. We are conscious of truths that were learned and accepted while we were on the lower planes. This plane represents hidden life, the reality of unspoken thoughts, feelings and emotions.

The **8th Plane** is the work of the Eight-Fold Path. The eight rays of this plane are Ego, Healing, the Path, Devotion, Knowledge, Imagination, Discipleship and Love. Here we receive training in setting aside the smaller self, discipline in overcoming self and circumstances.

The **9th Plane** is steeper going than the previous planes. This plane applies especially to walking in the light of understanding, the death and resurrection of the self in light and love. Spiritual balance, reality of message, discernment between imagination and revelation of truth, integration of spiritual power of sight and hearing are aspects of this plane. At this juncture, we depend more on ourselves, less on receiving outside help.

The **10th Plane** is the last plane on which we work as an incarnated soul. We unfold on the higher planes as discarnate souls. The action of the disciple on the 10th Plane is selfless life of consecrated service, the height of human earthly attainment brought into focus in service for the Kingdom of Heaven on Earth. Here are experienced the climax of growth, training of the ego, illumination, metamorphosis, and the development of spiritual balance.

There are hundreds, thousands of planes and heavenly dimensions beyond these first ten planes. We are given tests to pass on the spirals of each plane. These tests are personal, functioning to meet the need of each individual.

## MAP/CHART I – THE SUBPLANE/1ST PLATEAU OF HEAVEN

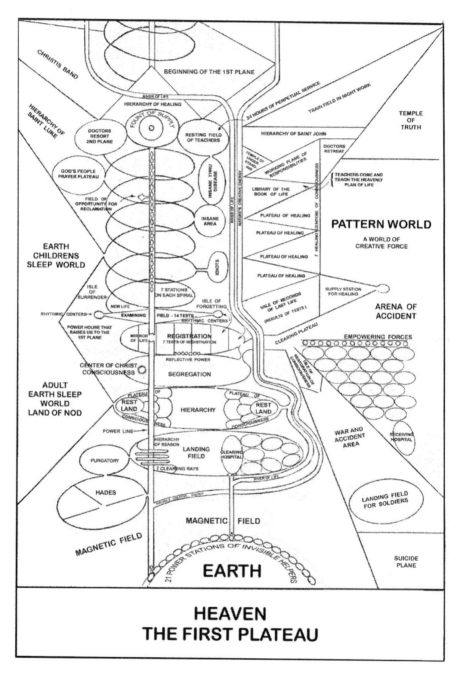

## POINTS OF INTEREST
## ON THE SUBPLANE/1ˢᵀ PLATEAU OF HEAVEN

Think of the two charts included in this book as maps beyond materiality as we know it. Here, we enter into the rays of power of creative energy that give light and growth. On the first chart you will find the following locations:

1. Earth
2. 21 Power Stations of Invisible Helpers
3. Suicide Plane
4. Nature's Creative Energy
5. Magnetic Field
6. Power line
7. River of Life
8. Hades (Hell)
9. Landing Field
10. Clearing Hospital
11. Landing Field for Soldiers
12. Plateaus of Responsibility
13. Seven Clearing Rays
14. Hierarchy of Reason
15. Purgatory
16. War and Accident Arena
17. War Receiving Hospital
18. Hierarchy
19. Two Restlands
20. Plateaus of Consciousness
21. Adult Earth Sleep World
22. Restoration of Consciousness
23. 21 War Hospitals
24. Segregation
25. Reflective Power
26. Center of Christ Consciousness
27. Empowering Forces
28. Registration - 7 tests
29. Isle of Forgetting
30. Results of Tests

31. Mirror of Life - Seven Tests of Registration
32. Clearing Platform
33. Arena of Accident
34. Examining Field - 14 Tests
35. Powerhouse Raises to First Plane
36. 2 Rhythmic Centers
37. Vale of Records of Last Life
38. New Life
39. Spirals, 7 Stations Each
40. Isle of Surrender
41. Supply Station for Healing
42. 3 Plateaus of Healing
43. Idiots (mentally challenged)
44. Earth, Children's Sleep World
45. Healing Centers of Consciousness
46. World of Creative Force
47. Pattern World
48. Field of Opportunity for Reclamation
49. God's People Prayer Plateau
50. Library of the Book of Life
51. Temple of Understanding
52. Working Plane of Responsibilities
53. Insane (mentally ill)
54. Doctors' Resort
55. Fount of Supply
56. Resting Field of Teachers
57. Hierarchy of St. John
58. Temple of Truth
59. Hierarchy of Healing
60. Spirals of Development (same as 39)
61. Training Field in Night Work

## CHAPTER TWO
## PICTURING REALITY BEYOND EARTH

To convey other dimensional reality from the standpoint of a three dimensional world is quite a challenge. To help us understand what lies beyond our lives on Earth, Mary Weddell's classes used unique detailed maps/charts showing the various planes, plateaus, fields, areas, temples, isles, islands, and other locations in Heaven as guideposts. Thinking of these maps/charts as illustrating states of consciousness, vibratory rates, and dimensions of being will give us a more accurate picture of Heaven as representing the different states and conditions through which an individual soul passes on the way to spiritual ongoing. The charts of Heaven included in this book can be thought of as maps of consciousness beyond materiality as we know it, and are useful to make a connection between the visible and invisible worlds.

Heavenly areas are made up of vibrations of energy from the coarsest to the highest refinement. As vibratory frequencies increase, these states and dimensions become less dense, increasingly refined and filled with more light. They represent the inner reality awaiting all who wish to know the meaning and purpose of life, here and hereafter. Each location beyond Earth is composed of variations of condition which may be designated as "strata," differentiated from each other by varying degrees of etheric refinement.

In her formative years as a clairvoyant, Mary Weddell studied with Charles Leadbeater, the prominent Theosophist who in turn had studied with Madame Blavatsky, and wrote of his experience and observations of the vibrations of the finely subdivided matter in nature. Aside from our recognition of matter existing in solid, liquid, and gas, Leadbeater said that in occult chemistry there is another, higher condition, the etheric. An atom of oxygen or hydrogen can be broken up, and by repeating the process, we find that there is one substance at the back of all substances. Continuing the subdivision far enough, we reach the unit which occultists call the Astral World. By further subdivision of that astral unit, we are dealing with another yet higher and more refined world. So far as we know, there is no limit to this possibility of subdivision, although there is a limit to our capability of observing it.

We can see enough to be certain of the existence of a considerable number of these different realms, each of which is in one sense a world in itself, though in another and wider sense, all are parts of one stupendous whole. These realms of nature we speak of as planes. In our study it is sometimes convenient to image them as one above another, according to the different degrees of density of the matter of which they're composed. However, this arrangement is merely adopted symbolically, and in no way represents the actual relations of the various planes. Nor should these planes be imagined as lying above one another like shelves, but rather as filling the same space and interpenetrating one another.

As Leadbeater says: "Every physical atom is floating in an astral sea of astral matter which surrounds it and fills every interstice in physical matter. The mental matter in its turn interpenetrates the astral in precisely the same manner, so that all these different realms of nature are not in any way separated in space, but are all existing around us and about us here and now, so that to see them and to investigate them, it is not necessary for us to make any movement in space, but only to open within ourselves the senses by means of which they can be perceived."

And now, in the words of our class:

**GEORGE FLOURNOY**  Can we take those thoughts further to better understand the nature of Heaven?

**MARY**  First of all, would we say we're looking at the "steeps of heaven?" Our Good Book speaks about going up, about being with angels in the upper realms of glory. It's interesting to take up our Bible and just look. Psalms, for one, over and over again. Can someone tell us one place we could go where there are six references in one book of the Bible that tells about the upper states of glory? In that, I think we have an explanation of Heaven.

**MARGARET BRANCHFLOWER**  Would that be the Book of Revelation?

**MARY**  Thank you, dear. I thought you'd answer. These are the things that give us a precedent, establish a basic foundation for building this thought.

You ask, what are the Planes of Heaven? They are expressions of the soul's growth and progression. And that is what we've been looking at down through the ages. We've been trying to build the story of the Earth and Heaven that it might be man's own. The Bible tries to build it. And in Revelation, John's vision probably was as clear as anything that was given. You can go into the Psalms of Solomon and find our teaching. In Joshua we can find points of it. There are many in the Old Testament, let alone the New; they are filled with it. They sing of the gladness of people all through the Old Testament. Now then, we go up to Areas of Consciousness there, like different lands. There are definite and distinct evolutionary steps to which an individual ascends in his progressive unfoldment.

The Heaven World: where are we at night? You have all wanted to know. Are we just sleeping? Are we in a sleep world? Are we picked up by teachers? We're told the heavenly temples are learning of the New Jerusalem. Most of our claims can be substantiated if you accept the Bible. If I go back into Egyptology, I would give a different method. For way back 8,000 years ago, the seers and prophets mentioned communication between the two worlds. It seemed a select few were given the power of mind, the development to combine the knowledge of two worlds. And from that knowledge were spun tales that came down through the ages, and so we have these "myths," as we call them.

**ESTHER BARNES** Mary, looking at the charts, these maps of Heaven, because of the limitations of the piece of paper, it looks as though the planes just rise one above the other. I know people would like to hear more about how the planes function in relationship to us here on Earth.

**MARY** I thought that our chart did it more gracefully than I could explain it. All right. After we leave this dimension of Earth, we briefly pass over a realm that is aerated, clear, vaporized, etherealized space with little activity or movement. From here we quickly enter the 1st Plateau/Subplane. As I see it, on the 1st Plateau, we're being given a glimpse into the Kingdom of Heaven, its reality, its perfection, its all-inclusiveness, where all is order, where love itself dwells, where tears are brushed aside, where healing abounds. This place was sought in earthly kingdoms but never attained.

It's easy to step into earth-like interpretations of the areas of Heaven and lose sight of a higher purpose and meaning that is activated by spirit, which becomes the fruits of love, and administers to all mankind regardless of race, creed or color – truly universal concepts. In the Good Word we read from the time we were children, they didn't give us much of a description of the land beyond this life. They told us it was beautiful; its streets were paved with gold, its gates were golden and "pearly." But many things are written too deep for us as Sunday School children to understand, and we found that there were various opinions, that no two really agreed. We wondered about those messages and visions the ancients received during their forty days in the wilderness. Would God remove a promise to his children that was prevalent back then, or would he continue at the same rate of universality now as it was then? Would we be deprived of a privilege of anything that earlier man had?

I'd be very satisfied to say to anyone who's ready to make their transition from this world to the next: you are not going into a place of fear, and you will be able to understand that land. Here, Earth is the shadow of the Heaven World. There, everything is proportioned and brought forward in the planes of life. There is a plan of life for this life here, just as there is a plan of life there, going on. When this life is over, we step into that next world into a new condition, new surroundings. Before we know it, we're comparing Earth with Heaven. And so, my conclusion would be that here we are living in the shadow land. Heaven was first. God was first. Creation was there, and it is here. It is truly one world without end, amen.

## CHAPTER THREE
## FROM THE SHADOW WORLD
## TO THE REAL WORLD
## ALIVE IN THE AFTERLIFE

**Snapshot**: When the newly deceased arrives at the Landing Field of the Subplane/1st Plateau, he is met by loved ones who are eagerly waiting there to greet him. We come under the care of the Hierarchy, who direct us to Restland for a period of seven days (and sometimes more), which in effect is rest plus adjustment and preparation. Following this we go to an area called Segregation Center, a place of revealing self to self, which poses testings and reflections from our lives, which leads to the area of Registration. Registration involves the Mirror of our Life and passing seven tests before we advance. Here is contained the life record we have established. On then to the Examining Field, where we take Fourteen Tests and where Rhythmic Centers are located, to give to us needed strength and stability. Next, Healing Areas and Healing Centers of Consciousness administer to the ills of body, mind and soul. Placing our own limits on ourselves, we are judged by ourselves.

**GENE HAFFNER** Mary, would you describe the process that happens to people in the transition of death?

**MARY** The silver cord is severed at death, as the soul, the eternal part of us, leaves the body and very briefly passes over the Rim of Life. The discarnate is led through woods by heavenly guides. As you walk through this primitive forest, you are impressed by its stillness and beauty.

Ahead, you see the River of Life. The entrance is from that primitive forest. And as man walks through this primitive forest, stirred by the stillness and the beauty of it, he reaches the River and steps down into it. It seems the natural thing to do. No one asks you to do it. You walk through and cross the River. As you step out of the water, you are washed clean and are perfectly dry.

Then you begin to climb a bit. You arrive on the Subplane/1st Plateau into glory, into the Kingdom of Heaven. It's an entrance filled with awe into that world at the Landing Field. Immediately, you see surroundings of amazing beauty and intensity.

**HANK**  Is there a very marked difference between that world and ours here in terms of flora and fauna?

**MARY**  In the Heaven World, we find landscapes similar to those on Earth, including trees, flowers, mountains, bodies of water, but everything is far, far more beautiful and ordered.

**CLARA JACKSON**  What happens as the soul arrives on the Plateau?

**MARY**  You begin to meet up with your own. Stepping up to the Landing Field, the soul is received by welcoming arms. You are always met by people who love you, usually parents who have predeceased you, and your sponsor.

**DIANA DAVIS**  Suppose your parents and even your grandparents are still alive and you're not? Who meets you then?

**MARY**  If you should predecease family members, it will be the great-grandfather or great-grandmother, whom you may not ever have known on Earth, who will meet you. There is that touchstone between yourself and Heaven. You are never forsaken. No man, woman or child comes home to God who does not receive a welcome with outstretched arms. People are often surprised to find so much love waiting for them.

**MIRIAM WILLIS**  I worked for many years as a nurse, and I well remember watching a dear patient experience her transition. As I watched, I saw the shadowy figures of her mother and father, her high guide and others beloved to her reach out their hands earthward over the River of Life, ready to receive her soul body as it gently left her physical body. As she passed through this River, her soul body was strengthened, her consciousness alerted, and joyously with recognition, she was fully received by her loved ones at the Landing Field.

**FRED ADLER**  Mary, you mentioned a sponsor. Who would that be?

**MARY**  He or she who sponsored you into the world. The sponsor is a great soul who through many lives has taken the responsibility of guiding and helping a particular soul or a number of souls.

**HANK**  Does every human being, however depraved, have a sponsor?

**MARY**  Everyone has a sponsor, yes. No matter how sinful or lost a person is, they have a sponsor. They are welcomed souls coming into the Kingdom, and God has the respect for that soul to give it entrance.

**LOLA GRUBE**  When we reunite with our loved ones, what do they look like? Do they look the same as we remember them at the end of their lives?

**MARY**  If they've been over there long enough, they appear to be in their mid-30's. That's my experience with the people I've been familiar with.

**ESTHER ESTABROOK**  I understand after a certain amount of time a person starts looking younger in Heaven. How long would it be before our loved ones on the Other Side appear in their prime again?

**MARY**  About ten years being over there. An elderly relative of mine who passed in her 90's a few decades ago looked no more than 35 when I saw her over there not too long ago.

**EVELYN SWANSON**  Would you speak more about the function of the Landing Field?

**MARY**  The Landing Field is a very beautiful area centrally located on the 1st Plateau/ Subplane, as you see on the chart, above the Magnetic Field. The Landing Field welcomes the traveler amidst a joyful atmosphere and gets us started in the direction we will next go, to Restland. This area helps souls become oriented to their new state of being.

**MARGARET**  So the Landing Field is exclusively for souls who've made the transition of death.

**MIRIAM WILLIS**  Yes, it is.

**LOLA**  What happens after the deceased arrives there?

**MARY**  The soul, having progressed to the haven of Restland, is now under the supervision of the Hierarchy, and is enlivened for seven days These first seven days are a grace period of love and understanding in which everything is pure ease, joy and happiness.

**ANDREW HOWE**  What does Restland look like? Could you comment on its appearance in terms an Earth person could relate to?

**MARY**  It's a land of beauty and true rest. There are beautiful meadows, arbors, pools, and enclaves; there is privacy. There are many condominiums and lovely quarters to accommodate people. Restland's purpose is orientation, recovery and rehabilitation.

**EMILY**  And this takes place over seven days?

**MARY**  Seven days is customary for most people, but if there's a need or desire to stay longer, they do. There's no coercion. Each individual sets his own pace, and may stay until the conscious mind is stirred to seek a higher attainment. Some reside here for fairly long periods before working upward to the higher planes. One can linger by choice, but if so, progress isn't being made yet.

**MIRIAM WILLIS**  Only when leaving Restland does spiritual progress begin.

**MARY**  After the seven days' grace period, the soul reverts to the level of consciousness it had at death; Earth consciousness overtakes it. If the person has been sick, he is in this state of consciousness. If paralyzed, he again becomes paralyzed, or rather, believes he is.

**MIRIAM WILLIS**  Suffering, wanting its old haunts, fighting or in shock or whatever the predominating consciousness was then prevails. The consciousness that had been so enlivened for seven days is forgotten, it becomes completely blotted out, obliterated to such an extent that some souls don't know where they are or what has happened to them.

**MARY**  They have lapsed back into the condition they were in when their life ended and now must go on to be healed for as long as it takes to clear them of the condition they have lapsed into – because they feel that is their reality, the reality with which they left the Earth.

**MIRIAM WILLIS** When the soul reverts to this condition, it goes to a suitable hospital or to the Clearing Hospitals on the seven Plateaus of Consciousness, to be helped to understand its situation.

**FRANK CRANDALL** What are the Plateaus of Consciousness?

**MARY** The Seven Plateaus of Consciousness serve as treatment and adjustment centers where one is oriented to the new life, helped to change to the rarer atmosphere of the planes of eternal life. The newly discarnate is given the utmost caring and love by guides. Helpers talk to them and try to give them an understanding of where they are, why they're here, and what they can do about it, placing the responsibility upon the soul itself.

**MIRIAM WILLIS** The clinging attraction of Earth needs to be cleared. Some people don't realize they've entered a different state, so they need to become conscious of it. Or perhaps they've done something they can't forgive themselves for.

**MARY** When nearing death, a person might have been fighting the fact that they had to depart this world and leave a family behind. That's something that has to be reckoned with. All these elements that bind us to Earth and make us long to come back must be erased.

**MIRIAM WILLIS** It's difficult to give up yearning for relatives or stop struggling to hold onto the life that's passed. For many, leaving things unfinished or to letting go of the things that were cherished in life isn't easy.

**MIRIAM ALBPLANALP** So people don't automatically find continual pure bliss in Heaven, but need to become accustomed to their new state.

**MARY** The departed are sometimes frozen in their attachments and fears. Some deceased grieve for their former lives and loved ones. These Earth states of consciousness receive skilled care and encouragement toward healing the scars and wounds, cleansing of

Earth consciousness. If you want your favorite chair, your favorite bed—it's automatically there. Everyone is given the opportunity to progress as desire is quickened within.

**MIRIAM WILLIS**  Some are so close to the physical body that they feel through the mental body all their old physical ills. Those who need time to recover from an earth illness or dysfunction spend a long time getting well, going through the clearing rays many times. The condition they had in their physical life lingers in their mind, and they need to overcome the mental and emotional effects.

**MARY**  The heavenly guides help them to understand what needs to be done, but it's the responsibility of every individual soul to pick up the load themselves. As that desire springs up in the heart, opportunity is given spiritually through the Seven Rays of Clearing.

**FRANK**  And they sometimes have to go through these over and over again, many times?

**MARY**  There are no limits in time ... as many times as it takes for the healing to be accomplished.

**MIRIAM WILLIS**  Rehabilitation means re-clothing a soul's consciousness, which can be quite a task for some individuals.

**MARY**  But there are always those seven days of grace, and everyone is given help in the most loving way.

**HANK**  I have a question. Many psychic mediums as well as people who've come out of Near Death Experiences report Heaven as being a state of never ending rapture, joy and peace. It's been my thought that these people are seeing the first seven days only, the heavenly grace period, but haven't ventured beyond. We don't hear much about anything after that; we don't hear that we have an accounting to deal with, that we all have work to do over there.

**LOLA**  I thought of that too. It seems to me that neither the mediums nor the near death people consider that point. They're basking in the wonderful initial after death experiences in Heaven without moving forward.

**FRED**  You mentioned that some people don't move on to the next step for a while until they choose to.

**VIOLET STEVENS**  You may remember I once brought back the memory of seeing my stepmother in a hospital. My stepmother spent several years in one of those hospitals before she got out of that obsession of being sick. She couldn't go on.

**MIRIAM WILLIS**  She was in Restland for some time.

**MARY**  No one is ever asked to leave Restland. You don't leave until you're ready. If the discarnate seems afraid to go on, if they've been in Restland too long, the Hierarchy works extremely hard to move them out. Because a person can become quite fixed where they are. Some will feel "just let me relax."

**MIRIAM WILLIS**  They're relieved and don't want to be bothered. They just want to take it easy, and that is certainly allowed. They just won't progress.

**HELEN VON GEHR**  Are there seven categories to be cleared, as there are only seven rays?

**MIRIAM WILLIS**  The Seven Rays complete the need.

**JEANNE REJAUNIER**  Would these seven rays correspond somewhat to the seven deadly sins?

**MARY**  Very much. You know, I feel there are so few of us in this class who have indulged ourselves in the seven deadly sins, that I feel we're don't need to cover that territory very much.

**GERTRUDE CLARK**  Would this also include people that are catapulted into the Other Side?

**MARY**  If they were catapulted in, they would go the accident way, would they not? Then the same form of things would happen to them.

**MIRIAM WILLIS**  And they will either go forward or stay for a long time and go through the different clearings again. The War and Accident Arena which Mary alluded to is on your charts.

**MARY**  The development of the soul depends on whether they take hold of life over there and absorb it, or whether they resist it.

**GENE**  You mention the Hierarchy. Who are they? What do they do, and what's their purpose?

**MARY**  The Hierarchy is a group of developed higher souls; we'll say they're from the $100^{th}$ Plane. They're living above our world today, from where they can see our problems, our future, our past. Remember, the Hierarchy are thinking minds the same as yourselves. Like us, they have lived on Earth.

**MIRIAM WILLIS**  It's a group of talented invisible teachers who know life here and hereafter, and are able to work both ways with equal ability. They are informed. The Hierarchy have the usage of the power, the lodestones of power and power stations through magnetism, as you will see on the chart.

**MARGARET**  Is the $1^{st}$ Plateau/Subplane roughly three-dimensional, or is it something else?

**MIRIAM WILLIS**  We're told not to try to estimate anything in regard to dimension over there. It's a different calculus entirely.

**BARBARA STONE**  I'm curious about time there. How do they reckon it?

**MARY**  There is no time as we know it. In the Heaven World, time is designated by that world, not our Earth time.

**LINDA CLARK**  But is their seven days the same as seven days here?

**MARY**  It's the twenty-four hour day. I merely use that because there's no other way I could designate. It isn't day and night over there. It's mid-day, sunrise, noon, and twilight, sundown, and then we live in the ray of a deep sunset. Through the night it is the twilight sunset, which is very beautiful.

**SYLVIA HOWE**  Sort of like the "land of the midnight sun" in our world?

**MIRIAM WILLIS**  Yes, indeed, and even more beautiful.

**LOLA**  It seems a bit odd that people who've lived exemplary lives, once they get over there in Heaven, are treated the same as people who've done incredibly terrible things in life. And yet these people are met by their loved ones, too.

**MARY**  If I were going over, my people would meet me. If you were going over, your people would meet you. That is God's world and God's plan. No man enters that world who isn't greeted. You're greeted with love no matter who you are. Criminals, thieves, murderers, you're greeted, and for seven days you're treated the same as the man who has lived the Christ life. That is the law of love that operates in God's kingdom. So each person is allowed a vision of what can be, and from then on, each person wherever they happen to be, is sought and given the chance to reveal their desires and go to higher realms. Just as surely as they desire, it will be given them. It happens both ways, whether the decision is to go up or to go down.

**ANDREW**  After one decides to go forward, how does spiritual ongoing proceed?

**MARY**  After death, one is handed two blueprints: what your life could have been and what your life actually was, and you begin to look at your Earth life under close scrutiny. Before advancing to a higher plane, there are preliminary areas: Segregation, tests, refinements in the Rhythmic Centers, Registration and the Mirror of Life all remind us of our shortcomings, unheeded truths and the lack of fulfillment in our lives.

**MIRIAM WILLIS**  Those who are imbued with the desire to go further advance to the Isle of Segregation, which on the chart is located at the left above the Hierarchy and Restland.

**GERTRUDE**  Are there specific requirements to enter the Isle of Segregation?

**MARY**  Those who come here have reflected on their lives and have reached into the power of consciousness to the extent that they know what's needed to go where they belong. In that Isle of Segregation, they're segregated from everyone else, alone with the teachers, where the teacher talks over their lives with them, their past, their future, their options. They analyze all the facts as to how they have failed, what they've gained, and what still needs to be accomplished.

**LOLA**  Would that be mostly regarding how they fell short of their ideal intentions in life?

**MARY**  There's emphasis on how the person has failed to measure up to the ideals he came into the world to express, his original Plan of Life. It's quite a problem to go through Segregation and not feel awfully wounded.

**MIRIAM WILLIS**  Again, what your life could have been and what it actually was.

**LINDA**  Can you ever argue with these higher beings? Suppose you disagree with their conclusions? Can you defend yourself?

**MARY**  You can try reasoning with the teachers; you're given that privilege. You see your life and what you can do to change. The teachers are seeing you as you really are. If you want an argument, there's always a teacher there who'll talk to you and let you try to make a case for yourself. But nearly always, you come back again in the same old surroundings, questions and answers. Often, you put up a straight argument about something and find that the teacher disappears and you're left alone with your thoughts. Then it's up to you to reflect and come to understand the lesson, and it's usually a very severe lesson to learn.

**CLARA**  Mary, would it be fair to say that none of these heavenly areas are geographical, but they're all levels of consciousness?

**MARY**  Well, they seem very geographical when you get over there, even though by our Earth standards it's a different order. We can say we "go up in the air." Before you know it, you see that these areas are peopled; that everything is organized, these areas all have buildings, and especially, on the Subplane, hospitals of all descriptions. There are cities just as we have here, only much more beautiful, serene, cleaner and more orderly.

**GENE**   Could you describe the heavenly areas, their temples, homes and other buildings, in terms of a certain number of feet of elevation above each other?

**MARY**   As I look up and I see the planes, their temples practically look as if they touched the sky. Of course the sky is the horizon and seemingly infinite. As far as the eye can see, the towers go way up. Feet —I couldn't tell you.

**ESTHER ESTABROOK**   Mary, is it difficult for human beings to make the transition to the other side? By that, I mean is it difficult to die and go over?

**MARY**   It isn't difficult to come over, but prior to dying, it may be stressful for some, thinking about what's waiting for them. If a man has no faith in the Afterlife and he's lying there waiting for his life to end, there's not much for him to look forward to. In the prelude to dying, many times the man with faith suffers as well. While he's lying there waiting for death to come, he's thinking of all the things that have been wrong in his life.

**MIRIAM WILLIS**   All that is lifted from you in the transition of death.

**MARY**   You are received into the Kingdom. You don't know any suffering when you arrive, any sin or wrong thinking. You're accepted. When people come to that side of life, the grace period may not last long, but through that period, they will always remember it.

**MIRIAM WILLIS**   Even spiritual people, so accustomed to the Earth, must become acclimated to the new life. Even the enlightened have something to overcome.

**MARY**   We continue to face all the challenges, the adversities, the trials and tribulations from our lives. We're accountable for what we do and don't do on Earth. We see and feel everything we did to others. We see the suffering, confusion, inequality, ignorance and cruelty of life on

Earth. Most of us die leaving unfinished business. Not everyone can accept this.

**MIRIAM WILLIS**  From Segregation we go into Registration. These are the Registration tests, are they not, Mary?

**MARY**  Yes, and this is where reincarnation may come in for those who are ready to look that far back. You can see that right through all your lives the same thing turned up over and over again. So you have your Mirror of Life in the Registration tests.

**GLENN DIES**  What happens in the Registration tests?

**MARY**  The Isle of Registration is divided into seven sections, including the Mirror of Life, where the self is truly reflected. You register your fears, your hatreds, your loves, everything is registered up there. We're shown our credits; we accept them at Registration. You first see some very positive things about your life; then it's as if they're turned over to the other side and you see something quite different. You were unprepared for what you see; the reality is quite astonishing. We feel we should have known better in the first place. In other words, what you see next is contrary to what you originally saw. You see its opposite, the way you expressed a quality in a negative way.

**MIRIAM WILLIS**  There's something about coming face to face with what you see in those mirrors. You initially want to disavow this could be you, but you recognize very quickly that the mirrors don't lie. You see it, you recognize it, so you accept it.

**JOHN #1**  Are the Seven Tests of Registration difficult to pass?

**MARY** Very difficult, and if you don't pass them, you just stay till you do. Yet you never doubt you've done any of these things when you once see them in the Mirror of Life. There's a continual movie as you watch. It goes through like a motion picture; you see your tendency to take what you want and cover up what you don't want. It's all written there in the mirror of your own life. You're responsible for everything from the age of seven on.

**ESTHER BARNES**  Does this procedure bear a resemblance to what some people refer to as the "life review"?

**MIRIAM WILLIS**  In many ways it does. When we look in the mirrors and see there were things lacking in the life just lived, it's often the things we leave undone rather than the things we've done. What don't you want to see or accept? What are you in denial over? What were you avoiding in life?

**MARY**  There are seven mirrors in the Registration tests, clear mirrors and black mirrors. You stand before them and see what was positive and what was detrimental to you on Earth. No one tells us. We see it depicted there in those mirrors. There are just as many things you did well. But when you step away from that mirror, there's no memory of what you've done that was right; it's what you haven't done right that you remember. Possibly the life of someone else could be affected by something that we deliberately did. At the time it didn't impress, but we have to forgive ourselves and forgive others.

**HELEN MARSH**  In making progress over there, you have to first want to, don't you?

**MARY**  You certainly do.

**LENORE**  So if they don't want to, not everyone will go this way?

**MARY**  Sooner or later, they will. Some will delay the reckoning, and that's allowed. Remember, you go at your own pace. You're the boss of your own consciousness.

**SYLVIA HOWE**  I'm looking at the chart. What are the Seven Lodestones of Reflective Power? What do they do?

**MARY**  Seven Lodestones of Reflective Power reveal our soul's attainments and shortcomings.

**MIRIAM WILLIS**  And after the seven tests of Registration, just above this, is the Examining Field with its Fourteen Tests.

**SYLVIA**  Could you please explain the Fourteen Tests in the Examining Field?

**MARY**  You're taking up the balances of why you had a particular trait. If you accept it, and you don't have to accept it, but if you do, you can see that right through your life these certain traits have shown up. Many times it's a negation, something that you just will not recognize or that you believe isn't worth recognizing.

**HANK**  Who does the examining?

**MARY**  That would be the sponsor who sponsored you into the world, the teachers that have helped you, and someone that is always from a very high plane. People have said to me they come from the 100$^{th}$ Plane and higher. You feel almost alone with yourself, yet these people are about you. Fourteen questions are asked. They vary according to the type of person, the advantages he had in cultural and educational values.

**MIRIAM WILLIS**  And you always have a second chance.

**MARY**  The Fourteen Tests must be reconciled before going on to the Powerhouse that raises one desiring higher consciousness into a higher plane.

**ANDREW**  What are the Rhythmic Centers? What is their purpose?

**MARY**  They're at the ends of the Examining Field of Fourteen Tests. If we have the Seven Tests of Registration and looked into the Mirror of our Life, we then enter the Powerhouse that raises us to the 1$^{st}$ Plane. Then we are given the Fourteen Tests on the Rhythmic Centers of our consciousness.

**JEANNE**  Someone who was trained in spiritual work, would they keep their consciousness?

**MARY**  They would keep their consciousness.

**MIRIAM WILLIS**  This brings to mind how beneficial spiritual development is in our Earth lives, because then we don't need to go to those hospitals, and we don't need to have all these long delays in any area after death. We focus on that here in our training, so that a good part of the work we would have had to do in the Afterlife has already been accomplished right here.

**VIOLET**  In our teaching, we're trying to clean things out, so that when we go over, we can advance more quickly. Whatever we have put in our mind and stored that's good, that is our treasure.

**ALMA JOHNSON**  Going back to the River of Life: on the chart, it looks like the River of Life is quite extensive, like it goes on and on, up through higher planes.

**MARY**  The River of Life flows through all the planes. It's a connecting lifeline from Earth to the Heavens. The River of Life is the powerline between ourselves and God. When one goes over, conveying you into that Kingdom of Heaven is that beautiful River.

**MIRIAM WILLIS**  It's the conduit that brings the newly departed soul to its higher dwelling place.

**EVELYN**  In mythology, there's a river known as Lethe, where life's memories are washed away; there is the River Styx, there's the boatman named Charon who ferries the soul across the river. When we go over from Earth to the Other Side, might there a boat and a boatman that propel us to heaven?

**MARY**  It will be a boat for people that have that concept, and many people do have that concept. They've seen the boat. It's like the Spanish sail, perfectly beautiful, the sunset when they went over. Others have said, I have no remembrance of how I went there, but it was not unpleasant. I've talked no end to people on the Other Side of their experiences. No two people seem to have had the exact same description.

**MIRIAM WILLIS**  I was with my mother when she was dying. It was a fairly long process. She said, "I can see the boat coming; it's in full sail and it's getting nearer all the time." Evidently she had the experience of the boat coming for her and she could see it.

**JEANNE**  My grandmother's last words were. "I'm going when the tide goes out." So she saw the transition of death in terms of water, too.

**GENE**  For us here on Earth, is it possible to tell how much time is left as a person nears death? I'm not talking about the physical signs that medical people observe. I mean, is there some spiritual sign, something that happens to the person's aura as they get closer to death?

**MARY**  All I could say is that, where I've been close to people in sickness, the gray of the aura warns me that time is getting shorter. As I see that, then I can pretty well figure the time. I've been with people as they passed where I've been able to see the gray blanket coming up over the head and out over the shoulders first, then extending down.

**ELLEN KING**  Do they alert you from the Other Side when a person is about to pass away?

**MARY**  From the Other Side, they would not tell me. I asked one time, wanting to know when someone was passing so I could be there. And they said, we cannot tell you; God alone gives life and takes life. And so I've never asked since. But I have felt many times in being around people I loved, I would see death creeping up in the aura, and that would convince me, because they do change.

**AVIS**  I lost a friend last Tuesday who knew she was leaving. I wasn't there, but she told another friend of mine, her niece, "I'm going; you needn't stay if you don't want to." And she told her niece that her discarnate brother was there with her. She asked if her niece could see him, and added, "He says I don't need to be afraid – he's come to take me over."

**MARY**  That's a great consolation,, isn't it? You know, we can be awfully alone at times, alone way beyond what the human mind conceives, until you arrive and you're welcomed with open arms into the Eternal Kingdom.

**HANK**  May I ask more about the work of the Clearing Hospital that's just off the Landing Field? Is that a place where they clear the consciousness of people who think they're still on Earth?

**MARY**  We have to become oriented when we arrive over there. At the Clearing Hospital, you receive orientation to go on. Say a person has had a very heavy stroke. They will be relieved of that stroke the moment they leave the earthly body behind and come into the seven day grace period in Restland. Then after those seven days, there's an adjustment to be made, because they carry the illness with them.

**MIRIAM WILLIS** Once that sickness is relieved from their mind, they can go on. We learn we have to leave our crutches, as it were, on Earth, to take up the real substance of our lives and face what we didn't face here.

**MARY** Sometimes it's a simple thing that holds you back. Pride is one of the greatest forces to overcome. We have so many various prides. So we have to deal with them – an envy of someone else we've carried; a subtle hatred for certain things we've carried through. These are things we pick up very quickly. The invisibles start working, the doctors and teachers start working on us, to first give us the clean spirit to pick up life there.

**JOHN #1** I'd like to mention, Mary, that apart from religious doctrine and belief and from our spiritual studies with you, there are decisive scientific theories for life after death.

**FRANK** That's so. Quantum theory can prove that life doesn't end when the body dies, that at death, consciousness moves to another dimension, a dimension beyond time and space.

**JOHN #1** The so-called "death of consciousness" exists in a person's thoughts only because people identify themselves with their body. They falsely believe that since the body perishes, their consciousness will disappear too.

**HANK** What they don't realize is that consciousness exists outside the constraints of time and space.

**FRED** It's consciousness that creates the material universe, not vice versa. Intelligence pre-existed matter. At death, energy is released from the body and your consciousness goes with it. So you're free of the physical body, but still alive in consciousness.

**HANK** In quantum theory, multiple worlds, multiple universes exist simultaneously, exactly as in our heavenly planes.

**GENE**  H.G. Wells posited this back in the 19th century in his story *The Door in the Wall*. That hypothesis was more recently developed scientifically by physicist Dr. Hugh Everett at Princeton, who has written about the theory of multiple universes.

**JOHN #1**  Everett explained there's an abundance of places where our soul can migrate to after death.

**ESTHER BARNES**  Exactly! As we well know! They migrate to our Planes of Heaven! And there are hundreds, thousands of these planes in Heaven.

**FRED**  Our brains are receivers for the consciousness that is intrinsic to the fabric of space-time. Consciousness is nonmaterial. It lives on after the death of the physical body.

**FRANK**  This explains things like Near Death Experiences, astral projection, out of body travel and reincarnation, without relying on any religious ideology.

**GENE**  So the energy that is your consciousness exists in your higher, spiritual body on another level of reality, until it's recycled back into the physical in a future birth, in reincarnation.

# CHAPTER FOUR
# THE OTHER FACE OF THE AFTERLIFE

### The Magnetic Field, Hell, Purgatory, and the Suicide Plane

**MARY** On the first map or chart, you find the Magnetic Field as well as Hell (Hades), Purgatory, and the Suicide Plane. We recognize these places because they do exist, but I'm not expecting to meet any of you people there.

**BILL JACKSON** How would we describe the Magnetic Field, and what's it like to be there?

**MARY** The Magnetic Field is a darkened area around the earth below the Landing Field, where earthbound souls and those still bound by negative attitudes and habits of drugs, alcohol, greed and corruption wander around in misery and unquenchable desire. These are souls who in their Earth life deeply negated God's laws, who suffer from the lack of spiritual enlightenment. We find murderers, avengers, utterly selfish beings, those who have been cruel in power towards mankind, all forms of deep sin, self-indulgence, and negation.

**BILL JACKSON** Why is it called the Magnetic Field?

**MARY** Because it's the most magnetic place you ever saw. People cling to anything because they're without footing, without a handhold, they're just there as people wandering. They grasp anything of Earth that they can grab onto.

**JACK SPAHR** This area is to the left of the Landing Field on the chart.

**ANDREW** There must be some sort of help for lost, abandoned souls like the ones who end up here.

**MARY** Help is given when the light of desire is felt in the soul. The door is never closed. Great ones volunteer to help any who wish to come out of the darkness, and every provision to rehabilitate and redeem is offered. All that's needed is the desire, and help is there. The Hierarchy in these Plateaus of Consciousness work harder on this side to come near. People who understand and know try to help the people who do not know.

**MIRIAM WILLIS**  This place is very dark, but it's more like a soupy, thick gray London fog. You can always see whom you're talking to. You can speak. Like attracts like, and you'll find little groups talking together.

**BILL JACKSON**  Isn't this area also sometimes referred to as "the other side of Restland?"

**MARY**  That's right. Our training is for the positive side of Restland, for people who have a firm belief and know where they're headed when they get over there. People who have a great deal to answer for are the ones who find themselves on this "other side of Restland." If they don't wish to be disturbed, they can wait right there until they decide to call for help.

**GEORGE**  I believe you once told us about an experience you had visiting the Magnetic Field. Could you describe that experience for us again, especially for the people who didn't hear it the first time?

**MARY**  In the Magnetic Field as we walked down there, there were gaming tables and a large group of people was gambling nonstop and forcing other people to gamble. In my personal experience in this lifetime, I've had virtually nothing to do with gambling dens and places like that, so this vibration was new to me. They showed us a roulette table, an actual table in an Earth casino, surrounded by avid crowds of people. The game was going on and the spirits were doing the work. These spirits were literally vicious. This is a picture I will not forget. That shows you what the Magnetic Field is, and the influence over people who are in the throes of gambling fever.

**LOLA**  You're saying these spirits were earthbound, they were hovering over Earth gamblers and influencing them, playing cards for them or calling out numbers, or helping people throw the dice?

**MARY**  That's how it was. It's from this Magnetic Field, the dark area, that discarnate people also come to Earth with ill intent or with added appetite, and increase the avidity of addicts to drugs, alcohol, thievery, murder – all these things.

**MIRIAM WILLIS**  It goes without saying that this is a highly undesirable area. But there is protection from the dark forces, according to the vibration of thinking, the outlook of a person.

**HANK**  Protection for those of us on Earth?

**MARY**  The Invisible Helpers form a protective band to the Earth. The dark forces cannot reach the Children of Light unless they're filled with fear, doubt, anger ... that's an invitation.

**MIRIAM WILLIS**  Or resentment, hatred, any of those things. These negative states lower the vibration, don't they, and expose one to the danger of dark forces.

**EMILY**  In the book *Life in the World Unseen*, the author tells how three of them under guidance went down into the gray world. There they went on into this horrible, murky, absolute darkness. They felt a terrible atmosphere, sensed the hideousness of the place they were in. They were told one reason why it was not dangerous for a person who knew how to move in that area, was that these people couldn't see any of them because their range of life was so low that there wasn't much expanse of light that they could respond to.

**LU ANN HORSTMAN**  How does a person get into a place so dark and murky and horrible?

**MARY**  It's according to their rate of vibration and the rate of vibration in the Magnetic Field. Some of those people are living very close to Earth.

**EMILY**  In this dark area, the author said these people are utterly vicious.

**MARY**  There are areas of the Magnetic Field that are very wicked, where the people are fighting relentlessly. The last thing that leaves those souls as they depart Earth is the fight for light for themselves. They are fighting for their selves.

**HELEN MARSH**  Do you think a great many people who are bound to these areas may have been taken possession of by obsessing spirits?

**MARY**  I don't know whether or not they're possessed or obsessed, but I've had that thought. We've said that many people have been able on Earth to clear others of obsession and alleged possession. I've only known the medical side of it. There have been some good cases through hypnosis I've known of. But I believe if we can live the Christ life and pray the Christ Prayer, the Lord's Prayer in earnest, we will redeem to some extent the vibratory activity of obsessions or whatever it is we speak of.

**PATTI**  Mary, as you talked about the activity in the Magnetic Field, I was wondering if a person were, for example, in Hell or Purgatory, is that person allowed by heavenly law to get down into the Magnetic Field?

**MARY**  Those from elsewhere who go into the Magnetic Field are teachers who are there to work. Groups of people go down as helpers. A man is never denied reformation, here or hereafter.

**PATTI**  But I was thinking of the people who come down to Earth and infill people with evil, craven desires and so on.

**JEANNE**  How do they get out of there to come down here?

**MARY**  Oh, my! They merge their personalities through. There are just as many powerful people in the world that have ruled through evil as for good.

**GRACE HALE**  About those people who are earthbound and in darkness, they can't cross the River of Life?

**MARY**  They have had that opportunity. When they first entered the Afterworld, they went through the River and into the Examiners' hands.

**JEANNE**  Even those who are earthbound?

**MARY**  They have had the pleasure of crossing the River, seven days in Restland, then through the Examining Field, and found that they needed to go back. There's nothing but justice in that world. Man finds his elevation in that world.

**JEANNE**   Before they made the decision to incarnate again and came to Earth, they must have been prepared to contribute something positive, and yet a lot of people haven't. How did they go so far wrong? Like Adolph Hitler, for instance.

**MARY**   You mention Hitler. Doctors whom I knew during wartime considered that he was a mad man, that he was not sane, that a power had twisted his mind. He had a design of his life that he almost worshiped, and he lived by it. I can't say where he went off, but he was a very ordinary person before he got this vision of what he was and who he was. We could say that he was wrong, that from the lower planes, entities were able, through his ambition and through his reaching out and drawing things to himself in a dishonest way, he ate up his own positive vibrations and made a nesting place for evil spirits. That is one of the things that we have been taught from that world there.

**JEANNE**   So, likely as not, when Hitler died, he went to the area on the chart designated as "Insane?"

**MIRIAM WILLIS**   Possibly, dear, but we don't know that.

**RICHARD**   Or he could likely be in Hell, I would say, although it's not for us to judge.

**VIOLET**   Mary, is it not true that a soul cannot move from one sphere to another without desiring to?

**MARY**   Yes. There's a vibratory activity between souls. If one were in the Magnetic Field and wanted to improve his lot, and a teacher came through who said, I wonder if you're ready to move on, and the answer was yes, then that person would go to the Examining Field, where they would be put before the big glass. They would see their own emotion, see whether the desire was reality or just a passing whim. If it was just passing, this person wouldn't be able to make his way in the Examining Field again for a period of time. But he still would have another chance. Man is never deserted. On the lowest plane toward Earth, the teachers go down there and talk to those people and ask them if they would like to reform, if they would like to change their lives and their outlook.

Opportunity is never taken from a person, but it can be a slow grade up.

**GENE**  I would like to ask a question about ghosts and haunting spirits. I accept that they're real, but I wonder why their presence isn't full scale on a constant basis all the time, instead of coming through in spurts.

**MARY**  These haunting spirits are not conscious all the time. The trip back takes too much energy. So they're oblivious for a while; they recoup, then they come back.

**GENE**  I'm also curious about Purgatory.

**MARY**  Purgatory is the place of understanding. There would not be a Purgatory if it wasn't for what men think.

**LOLA**  Suppose a church body had as part of its teaching the thought of Purgatory, that everyone has to go to Purgatory and be prayed out. Would a soul automatically go there because they were taught that way?

**MARY**  No. If a soul asked for prayers to be released from Purgatory, it would be because it has been a physical thing that they believed. At the same time, many physical things we believed are not with us after we get over there.

**LOLA**  I know relatives pay many times to have dear ones prayed out of Purgatory.

**PATTI**  I believe it is not "prayed out of Purgatory" but "prayed through Purgatory."

**MARY**  The prayers are to pray the soul through Purgatory.

**PATTI**  Catholics believe the soul passes through Purgatory and either stays there or goes on.

**JEANNE**  Mary, in the successive lives of people, do you think most people in their incarnations at one time or another probably had been in Purgatory?

**MARY**  I wouldn't know, dear. Really, they don't answer questions like that to common people like me. I've asked all your questions; I don't believe you could miss one that I haven't asked.

**ANDREW**  I've always heard that great clouds of negativity fill the area covering both Purgatory and Hell.

**MIRIAM WILLIS**  As well we would expect.

**MARY**  Hades, as some call it, or Hell, the term preferred by others, is a section all by itself, with different levels of understanding. That's the way it was given to me.

**LOLA**  Hell is the deepest pit, they say.

**ALMA JOHNSON**  In the Catholic Church, they pray for souls in Hell.

**MARY**  From the Other Side, they told me that's a redeeming feature; our prayers help the discarnate, even those in Hell.

**LOLA**  As I understand it, people in Hell are not lost forever; you can penetrate that.

**MARY**  True, but the element of desire must be there. The Teachers tell me there are souls living there without hope, with little desire to leave, just living on. They don't know whether they will come back in another round of life; they have no concept of what God's laws are. These teachers are greater than we can ever imagine, but they still don't know. I asked questions and could not get answers, so I have no answers for you. You know the Christ life and you know the straight way. You know "doing unto others."

**EVELYN**  Have you actually visited Hell, Mary?

**MARY**  I've been there, and I've seen a suffering far beyond anything you will ever know. I needed to see it. All right, there's no fire burning, but the heart of man is seared with the terrible sorrow of not being able to undo the things he has done wrong.

**SYLVIA**  Was going to Hades – Hell, difficult to tolerate?

**MARY**  The experience of going to that area is about the most unpleasant thing you can remember in your consciousness. Everyone who gets past the 7th Plane will have the experience on the Other Side of going down there and coming back with a real idea of the place. Then you really have it in your consciousness, and you understand much more when you intercede in the life of another person to keep them from dwelling in a state like that. Hell is what we think and what we do. Hell is involved within our own consciousness. They speak about the fires of Hell. Those in hell suffer terribly, but when I went to Hell, I did not see fire. Perhaps the burning desire to be righted of all wrong; perhaps the burning desire to create a life that we have taken creates a fire within.

**MIRIAM WILLIS**  Man has the chance here on Earth to undo because our life has been so given the privilege of asking and seeking to find the cause of it, removing the cause.

**ROWENA**  Is it the area where Jesus came to when he passed out of his body – wasn't he supposed to have visited Hell? There are accounts that he did.

**BERNARD BURRY**  When Christians say the Nicene Creed, we say, "He descended into hell."

**MARY**  I believe the whole of the Kingdom over there has seen our Christ. Many great teachers that work go down to those parts. I remember the story of one Hindu teacher who went down and did a great deal of good.

**DIANA**  I've led myself to believe there is no Hell but what we create in ourselves, and on the chart we see Hades. Would you interpret that for me?

**MARY**  Yes, because there is "Hell", as there is "Heaven," but not a fiery furnace. I'm going to tell you that after we've gone to the Hall of Records and received the pictures of our life and what we've done to someone else, we suffer a fire of regret. But as far as the fires of Hell are concerned, there is a degeneration in the human soul, and it goes to the very length where you'd feel there's no chance. But we who are in this work today believe that the Law of Reformation is never closed. Somewhere along the way somebody reaches out a hand.

**MIRIAM WILLIS**  In Hades, they fight the battle of wit. Then they tire of it and there is a great silence. They say that in Hades, they oftentimes ask to go back for a few days. That is the first spark divine, we say, that would be an indication to a teacher that maybe they're going to change their ways.

**ELLEN**  Isn't the region located below the Magnetic Field even darker?

**MARY**  The region that is darker than the Magnetic Field, the deepest one, is the Suicide Plane, where people never see each other and call out constantly. It's an eternal calling and calling. That is darkness, because they're in a fog there, wandering until the years of the Earth life would have been up. My greatest sympathy goes out to a suicide. They have to reclaim their life because they have taken it. They are cut off from God and his light.

**LOLA**  But surely, there has to be some hope for them.

**MARY**  It's a land of no return until the end of the Earth life would have been. And you do walk in a fog.

**MIRIAM WILLIS**  You're calling, you hear voices, but you make no connections until what would have been the end of your life on Earth.

**MARY**  So even if you don't want to stay on Earth, do not take your life, because you might as well be here; there's no happiness there. Now if everyone understood that, they wouldn't go through that sad time.

**EVA TOTAH**  I understand how suicide isn't a solution to the misery of the person who opts for killing themselves, but being on the Suicide Plane sounds so harsh.

**SANDRA**  Maybe it's a lesson they need to learn, and they couldn't get it any other way. Would being an old soul make things different? Could they get out sooner?

**MARY**  I'm not God, and I don't know his plan for the soul. If the soul is an older soul, maybe that soul is released sooner; I wouldn't know. But the thought that they gave us in the temples as we studied the suicide world, is that the taking of the life seems to be the greatest sin against our Father of anything that we can do. Because you have cut the connection between yourself and God. They say there's no greater sin than cutting ourselves off from him.

**CARMEN AUSTIN**   Does prayer help them when they're in the Suicide Plane? I remember a case of suicide that you and I prayed for.

**MARY**   Prayer helped. It was it a case of not a desire to take their own life but that party was practically out of his mind when he attempted it. Prayer once a day for the Suicide Plane is a must, if we really are Christians. We're told that intercessional prayer is something we can use. Let's take it. And whenever you're down and out and feeling sorry for yourself, pray for a suicide, because you're not facing what they are.

**SYLVIA**   How would you utilize this information with people who were very suicidal? How would you go about approaching them?

**GLENN**   I was wondering the same thing as Sylvia. How could we convince a person here on Earth not to commit suicide?

**MARY**   Tell them anything you think will help them. I went to a girl who was going to commit suicide. I did not do her any good at all. She went to the hospital, they pumped out her stomach. She didn't like me because she lived. In the end she became friendly but she didn't think I had any right to interfere. It isn't easy if a person is bent on suicide.

**JEANNE**   Do any of the people on the Suicide Plane ever see each other?

**MARY**   They're in a constantly moving fog and just hear voices.

**GENE**   How can you know when your Earth life would have ended? I'm thinking how this might affect a person contemplating suicide, if they could tell in advance how long they'd have to wait in the Suicide Plane before they got out.

**MARY**   God alone knows those things. We've seen over and over again there's no one set, infallible rule for predicting death.

**GENE**  It couldn't be a certain number of years, because it's so different for different people.

**MARY**  I have no knowledge there, and I wouldn't try. Besides, I don't know the end of my own life. I wish I did. And I certainly don't know the end of another person's life.

**GENE**  Do we have a preordained time to live here on Earth?

**MARY**  I can't answer that. According to doctors, I wasn't expected to live this long. I've been ready to make my exit gracefully for some years, yet I'm still here. So it must be ordained that I stay.

**ANDREW**  I was wondering if mercy couldn't operate in certain instances. A person who had cancer and is a great burden to the family, a great expense, takes his life.

**MARY**  We would have to look to the great justice of God for that. I couldn't tell you.

**RALPH**  For those who try to commit suicide and don't succeed, what kind of a karma do they have?

**MARY**  There's no karma to it if they live on. Karma is what you make. Yes, you come with karma. You wouldn't come into the world if you didn't come with a background of having to clean up a past life and go forward with the life you live.

**VIRGINIA**  A friend of mine was going blind, another had cancer. Both of them would have died within the year. In less than a year I met both of them on the Other Side of life. I asked them about rehabilitation. They said it takes a long while to get power back to belong to God's Kingdom again.

**LENORE**  Suppose someone committed suicide by virtue of being lured into the act by being possessed by another?

**MARY**  God is just; all justice would be given that person.

**FRED**  What happens when a suicide is ready to come out of the Suicide Plane?

**MARY**  At the time that a suicide comes out, there's a welcoming group. They're always happy to welcome the person who was a suicide who has finished their term of walking in the mist. And try to remember this always, when you're thinking of that world, there's never any condemnation. There's a place for you to wait; there's a place for you to sink lower; there's a place where you give nothing and you get nothing.

**LENORE**  What decides how long a suicide would walk in that mist?

**MARY**  God himself decides. I don't think I've ever heard any teacher give any information on that.

**JEANNE**  Do the suicides have heavenly teachers with them?

**MARY**  Yes. They have teachers who go in and try to help, try to comfort and give understanding.

**GRACE**  What about a person giving up his life as a noble gesture to help someone? Or committing suicide because you don't want to be a burden? Do they go to the Suicide Plane too, and maybe come out earlier?

**MARY**  Under the Hierarchy, they would find their place. From the time you enter that world, you will find the law of justice operates. You are receiving just what you deserve. We can see plainly why you've been criticized over there. If you're talking in the wrong place, entering the wrong place, there's a light that comes down and a voice says do not enter here. People investigating over there haven't any rights until they're told they have them.

**GRACE**  With regard to suicide, can some people who are in dire circumstances be excused?

**MARY**  Anyone who takes their life because of disease, you have a great sympathetic understanding, if nothing else. We're in no position to judge; we have to trust heavenly justice.

**LENORE**  Someone close to me made a suicide attempt. I prayed as I stayed right there with her in the hospital. I stood at the foot of her bed and asked the teachers and loved ones to help her, to pull her through, because it was a question whether she'd awaken out of it or not. She said afterward, "I saw you standing at the foot of my bed, but who were all those other people around you?" She even told me how some of them were dressed.

**MARY**  That was the proof of your prayer.

**LENORE**  When she came out of it, I told her these things you're talking about, about what happens to suicides after they're dead, and she said, "If I had known that before, I wouldn't have tried it."

**CARMEN**  Someone wanted me to stay with a friend who was threatening suicide. She was an alcoholic and I didn't know it. The next day she committed suicide. I couldn't feel exactly at fault, but it's still it is in the back of my mind.

**MARY**  Alcoholics have a difficult time. I've seen them come into the hospital or clinics, get treatment, go home, and there they were again. Sobriety was not their choice. I'm not saying I don't have a responsibility to everyone that has a need; we all do as Christians, but I cannot carry them unless they'll carry their share of the load. I can't shoulder all the load, nor can you.

# CHAPTER FIVE
# THE WAR AND ACCIDENT ARENA

**VIOLET**   While we're still on the Subplane/1st Plateau, we haven't mentioned the Accident Field yet.

**MARY**   Look at the map. On our chart of the Subplane/1st Plateau, just below the Pattern World is the Arena of Accidents. The Accident World is not far out; it's close to Earth, as you can see on the map. Emergencies are ministered to, then the accident victim is taken to the hospitals shown below. You'll notice that the War and Accident Arena is located here, together with another Landing Field specifically for war and accident victims.

**MARGARET**   Mary, do the people who come over to the War and Accident Arena have to wait before they go to Restland? Do they go through their Clearing Hospitals first?

**MARY**   Everyone goes to Restland first after they've passed over. No matter who they are, they have that seven day grace period.

**SANDRA**   What's the purpose of the Clearing Platform?

**MARY**   It's an area where souls in the War and Accident Hospitals are further healed in consciousness. There is a Receiving Hospital plus twenty-one other hospitals on the 1st Plateau. Invisible helpers pick up the souls from accidents and war. Victims will go back over and over and over again to where the accident was. They go to the hospital and Restland, then they go back to the scene of the accident, and back again to Restland and the hospitals.

**MIRIAM WILLIS**   And on the chart, here's the Area of Consciousness. When people need help to have the horror of what sudden death has inflicted upon them cleared from their consciousness, they're ministered to in such a way that healing takes place, they're cleared of the terror and the horrors and the association until finally all that is obliterated from their minds entirely.

**RUTH THOMAS**   I understand that many of our young men who were killed suddenly in war, when they're over there and are taken to the War and Accident Arena, they don t realize where they are, and they wish to return to the battlefield. They want to be in an Earth vibration again.

**MARY**  Oh, yes.

**RUTH**  Well, could they keep them there?

**MARY**  No, but as we said, they return them many times. It's according to what's good for that soul. They treat them with different healings, depending on each individual case. The Hierarchy sends healers over to work with them. It takes time to go back and see the battlefield, as well as their former home and their families.

**RUTH**  How do the invisibles bring the soldiers back to where they really are now? Do they go willingly?

**MARY**  They know before they go that they can't stay. They're prepared for that. There is no force used to impel them to come back. It's sometimes difficult, but they manoeuver.

**MIRIAM WILLIS**  Often soldiers go out fighting and they still think they're fighting. Soldiers who keep fighting sleep half the time.

**RUTH**  Then they allow them to sleep longer and give them the opportunity of going into the hospitals?

**MARY**  Yes. Then they can move from one group to another. They find different interests, and eventually somebody gets into that consciousness and finds what they can do to inspire the soul to go on.

**MIRIAM WILLIS**  The soldiers have established the magnetic mechanism whereby they can go back to that spot of accident or death. It's just above the Isle of Restoration of Consciousness, as you can see on the map.

**EMILY**  My question is about the area in the lower right hand corner of the map. Suppose one of our loved ones has suffered a fate of sudden death. Is there any special way to help our people who die suddenly as accident or war victims, and if so, how?

**MARY** What we would do on Earth is not what would be done over there. If we called for the Invisible Brotherhood, we would alert them to whomever it was that we had received word about. We'd alert teachers on the Other Side, calling the invisible helpers. It would go through the Hierarchy and we would see results.

**HELEN FLATWED** Could we ask in our night work to be taken to that hospital where this one was?

**MARY** I think not. They're in a state of shock. That world is organized. You could say, at some time in the future would you make it possible? Then you would be alerted; I would be alerted and you'd have your opportunity. You would not be refused as long as that person wanted to see you, unless they'd gone in shock and hadn't recovered their spiritual mentality.

**GEORGE** But isn't it true we as a class are being trained in our night work, so that sometimes we may be called to assist the invisible helpers who are working with the war and accident victims?

**MIRIAM WILLIS** Yes, indeed. The thing that I feel is very wonderful is the marvelous provision for every kind of need you can think of exists in the Heaven World. For instance, take the Landing Field for Soldiers. Would it be right to say that it seems as though the conditions of Earth have almost made this a necessity? That God has provided it because man has needed it so badly.

**HELEN** I know it's already been asked, but I want to ask further about helping our loved ones who die in accidents or are war victims. It wasn't clear to me what we could do, if anything, to help them.

**MARY** First of all we would have to orient ourselves with the condition in which they left us; we would have to have information how they passed. We could immediately lift into prayer for that person. We could enlist friends: I've lost so and so or my friend's son has gone over, and would you mind taking five minutes of prayer with me? Name the person, stay five minutes. Prayer is a petition sent forth from the human heart to the heart of God. Take it just that way. It isn't just a mass of words. It might also be singing a hymn. Music is very effective a prayer petition, as it invokes the heart.

**MIRIAM WILLIS**   Sometimes Earth people can understand and clarify the consciousness of these peoples' condition because we're close to the Earth vibration.

**JEANNE**   If a young man is killed and he's very young, like 19 or 20 with his whole life ahead of him, does he seek to have children over there?

**MARY**   I don't know anything about that, dear. Really I can't answer that, because I have no knowledge. I know that at first they group together in homes. In this one area – for instance, let me say, we were taken to barracks where they were staying. These barracks were clean, made of beautiful material, but rather barren. And that's where many of us are taken to help with the work. Usually those who are there don't stay long. They're moved on.

# CHAPTER SIX
# VISITATIONS, COMMUNICATION AND CO-MINGLINGS BETWEEN HEAVEN AND EARTH

**GENE**  We know that many a person from the Afterlife returns to their own funeral services. Is that something that's approved of, returning to Earth right after death?

**PATTI**  Sometimes people say they see the person at their funeral. Other times they don't. Is it a matter of choice whether we attend our own funeral?

**MARY**  Nothing is denied.

**MIRIAM WILLIS**  Some people understand they really are dead and decide to stay where they are in Heaven. Others ask to go see their homes back on Earth.

**MARY**  My experience has been that those who wish to attend their own funeral are always granted that privilege. Their loved ones on Earth would be very pleased if one they loved should attend their own funeral. At the same time, we need to release them to their new life.

**JOHN BRANCHFLOWER**.  Is it possible that many people aren't aware that they have a funeral to go to, that they don't realize they're on the Other Side?

**MARY**  Well, we did say that at first after death they're normal people, as they were on Earth. They remember Earth as if it were yesterday. If they've been sick a great while, they remember back as far as they were when they were in good health. Some people would still be tied to their Earth lives and know about a funeral. To others, this would not be an important factor.

**KATHY**  I've always had the feeling that people on this Earth and those who have gone over co-mingle, to an extent depending on their development.

**JOHN #1**  You got me to thinking about something. A couple of months ago I was sawing limbs off a tree in the back yard. I was using a saw that my father-in-law had given me. And I remembered when I was a kid I didn't know how to use a saw, so every time I would dig into a piece of wood, the saw would go in sideways, would buckle and wouldn't saw anything. And I would start over again, with my dad helping me cut the tree. Now, sawing the tree a few times recently, I could feel my dad's presence, I realized it was my dad who was helping me move my arm to make sure that the saw went straight. He couldn't work too long—couldn't sustain it, but it did happen a few times. And the tree got cut.

**HELEN MARSH**  Whenever I feel the presence of a loved one come through from the Other Side, it happens suddenly and unexpectedly. It's totally spontaneous and happens so quickly. I feel such a strong influence, especially right at the beginning stage of a visitation. I'm flooded with a fullness of recognition and an immense, overflowing love shared with that person. There's never any doubt who has come through; I know instantly in a flash of intuition, well before I have any time to think. It never lasts too long, because as John says, they can't sustain it.

**MIRIAM WILLIS**  Let's not forget that in our night work in the temples, we're able to see our loved ones over there as well.

**MARY**  We have the wonderful opportunity to see those we love on the Other Side in our night work if we arrange it. It has to be asked for. If we don't love anyone enough to want to see them, it certainly will not be suggested that you go and see them. But if there's anyone on that side of life whom you want to know that you recognize the things they did for you in the past, that's a good time to speak to those people and say thank you for what you did in my life.

**SYLVIA**  It's very interesting that you have to ask to see someone.

**MARY**  I feel it's no more than the right thing to do. I know the order of that world. Certainly if I wanted a book at the library, I'd go up and ask for it. So I go to this "information bureau" over there and ask for that person. After a certain length of time, the vibratory activity of that world would enter my consciousness and I would know when to go back, and they will set a date. I enter a solarium-like room, a beautiful place. And there that person is sitting waiting for me.

If you folks could just once bring back the vision of what it means to mother, father, sister, brother, aunt, uncle, grandparent to see us, to know that we're living. I remember an aunt I saw one time maybe 10 years ago. She went over when I was a young woman. She took me in her arms and said, I can't imagine your being so white haired and so old. She was my father's aunt. She was elderly when I knew her on Earth. Here I was, looking up into a shining face of a woman, maybe 40 years old or even younger. She was so sorry for me because I was so old. I never had remembered her young, of course.

**MIRIAM ALBPLANALP** You said the aunt took you in her arms. Are we in the kind of a body where we can embrace someone over there?

**MARY** Our spiritual bodies go toward each other and we can embrace each other. Love is expressed there.

**MIRIAM WILLIS** Many people are most anxious to speak back. And to hug.

**ANDREW** We should mention that it works both ways; those on the Other Side visit us here on Earth. The majority of "familiars," though, need a higher soul like a teacher to support them. They don't have the power to come back on their own, or at least to stay here very long.

**MARY** I've known very few people still on the 3$^{rd}$ Plane but what love the thought of touching the Earth and coming back here. Under those circumstances, we say we help them, and different bands help them, so they return to Earth and see their old haunts as they now are. Then they're told, when you go back again, remember, you have regular "information bureaus" that you can come to. You'll appear on such and such a day and you can be taken, if this is your desire. What are you going to do in return for it? In God's world, you're not given anything unless you take a stand for what you want, and earn it.

**ALMA** On the subject of visitations, Mary, out of curiosity, when did you begin to see discarnate people from the Other Side?

**MARY** Well, I think I was able to see invisibles from the Other Side for quite a while, but it wasn't quite the thing that was being done, and I was rather withdrawing from that. Remember, I knew a great deal about sickness in sanitariums; I lived in hospitals and sanitariums. We had a big government-established affair, an army hospital connected with Fort Lewis. My husband, Dr. Weddell, was the surgeon. They brought a patient in, a young man, and walking behind him I saw two women. I believe, tracing back, it was the first experience I shared with another person. This nurse was grumbling that she should be helped, so I offered to help her and got on the other side of the gurney she was wheeling the patient in on. I turned around. There were two women, plain as could be. I made some remark about the two women that the nurse ignored.

**HANK**  Two women from the Other Side, you mean?

**MARY**  That's right. We got the boy to the place where he had to go, the nurse was given a call, and she said to me, "Before I go, I want to tell you that I also saw the two ladies. One was middle aged and the other was young." And she told me we'd have a talk about this some day. She reached out in the kindest way and said, "I will never tell anyone, and don't you either." That was quite consoling. After that, I was seeing so many around these boys. A good many deaths were occurring there.

**MIRIAM WILLIS**  What about Fred, Mary? Tell us the story of your brother Fred.

**MARY**  Oh, I did have an experience I believe was one of the most convincing. We had a great shaggy dog at our house. The kitchen floor was marble, old-fashioned black and white marble, newly polished to perfection. It was raining out. Father was visiting a sister whom he hadn't seen in many years, and Mother was upstairs in bed recuperating from an accident, having been thrown from a car. I came downstairs and found that the dog had pushed open the kitchen door and was making himself at home on that nice clean floor, and was he muddy! He'd been under the car, for another thing.

I ordered him, "Get out of here!" but he didn't move. Well, I was dressed to receive company, and the dog refused to budge, and there was no one to help me. I stood there for a moment, and thought, I've got to get this dog out of here. If he goes upstairs he'll jump all over the boys' beds. And I was quite distressed. So I went to the door and pretended as though I had something for the dog to eat. This dog always wanted to eat. I called him by name and went outdoors with the food, and when I came back in, I saw a shadowy figure standing on the other side of the fireplace.

**GLENN**  I remember that fireplace, Mary. It was an old-fashioned fireplace with kettles in that kitchen.

**MARY** That's right, Glenn. And over there was a shadowy form. But something had to be done about that muddy floor. So I went quickly and put on an apron. I took Ivory soap flakes, a dishpan of water and a big sponge that they washed the cars with, and got down on the floor. I'd washed many floors, but you take Ivory soap and wash a marble floor, and people nearly always skid because you can't get the soap up. I got plenty of soap down, and I was carrying one pan of water after another. And soon I became tired. I was sitting back, looking at the floor that was shiny like a mirror. And there was my brother who had passed out in wartime, the eldest brother, and he was standing there smiling.

I said, "Oh, Fred! Why didn't you wait to come until Mother was well?" I felt a wonderful joy seeing Fred again. And he said to me, "Mother's going to be all right, but you'd better get a rug for the floor and put it down." Well, I took Fred's suggestion; I put a rug down, one of those braided rag rugs, and swished it around over the floor. It dried things pretty well.

The next Thanksgiving, when we were all at home, was to be the first Thanksgiving without this brother that had gone on. We had many guests for dinner, and Fred appeared again. My sister said, "Oh, do you see Fred? Oh, Fred's here! Isn't it wonderful to have Fred here!" Father, quite overwhelmed, said, "Yes. yes, yes." Other people at the table were scared to death; something like this just wasn't being done. My cousin Lloyd turned stark white, got up and left the table. Two or three others left the table as well. Mother told Father, "You'd better go out and see if they're all right."

**VIOLET**  You saw your brother Fred, but your guests didn't.

**GLENN**  Everybody in the Dies family saw Fred – Mary, Mother, Dad, our sister Tasma, our brothers Paul and Ed and I all saw him.

**MIRIAM WILLIS**  The whole Dies family were sensitives.

**MARY**  In my teaching, I've said to each person, don't take my word for it, please. Prove it for yourself. Take your colors and climb that Channel until a face, a teacher's face, a guide's face or a loved one's face looks through. And then be satisfied that you have proved the life beyond. Take the word, then, and let it come back you. If I do nothing else, if I have served one person to take away the fear of death, then I've been given something. I call that seership, and I feel it's one of the greatest fields of work. Every gift you can give by proving or sharing – I almost feel it should be stated in a whisper.

I believe we're here to learn lessons. We're in school for this day, and it is a very short day. Life is never long enough. I'm perfectly sure that if you saw the sketch of your life that was given you when you entered this world, you'd know you could never live long enough to fulfill it. And as you get to be elderly – my age – most elderly people that love God will say the days pass so fast, they don't feel able to accomplish anything!

**GEORGE**  Thank you; it was very interesting.

**JEANNE**  One of the spirits you've spoken of whom you knew who was killed in World War I was Raymond Lodge, the son of Sir Oliver and Lady Lodge, and he's been very much on my mind lately. I don't know why; and also Lu Ann asked me about him about a week ago. I found it interesting that we were both thinking about him.

**MARY**  Let me see. There was a book, *Raymond*, that someone passed to me, but I didn't get to read it, because someone borrowed it. I went home one day and there was that book on a telephone table. I picked it up and thought, I don't remember that I was given that book back. Where did it come from? But my name was in it.

I wondered who returned the book! I was living across Lake Washington in a country home district, up north. It was not only chilly, but rain for Seattle was predicted. We planned to eat dinner outdoors, our first big meal of corn that season. We had invited several people over to eat corn. I was standing tending it, and someone asked, "What kind of corn is it?"

I looked behind me, and there was a young man standing there. Well, it could have been anybody's son, because you never knew who was going to come to those outdoor affairs. And I said, "Oh, it's Sir Phillip corn. It's really for horses, but we love it!" And he asked, "Did you know my father was coming to your area?" I said, "I don't know who your father is," to which he replied, "Sir Oliver Lodge." I had heard Sir Oliver lecture; he had been to Seattle a number of times, and I'd heard a great deal about him, because many other people, if they went to England, always made it a point to hear him lecture. And Sir Arthur Conan Doyle was another one, a great friend of the Lodges, who had also lost a son due to injuries in the war. My friends would come back and tell me about the lectures. So I was acquainted with what the Lodges believed.

And this young man said, "I want you to write my father and tell him you saw me." The young man disappeared and we served the corn. I didn't seem to be able to swallow, I got so worked up about that incident, thinking what in the world am I getting into? I went inside the house, and the young man was sitting in there. I supposed he just appeared. He wouldn't have the power to stay any great length of time, you know. They never do. And he said, "I have left my father and mother's address. You write to Lady Lodge, my mother, and tell her that when they visit Seattle on the 10th of next month, I want them to come and see you, because no one has seen me as clearly as you have." That was a revelation to me, because I didn't think I could see anybody any more clearly than anyone else could.

So I took that address, Normantown House, Buildington Way, and the number and everything. I'd been told this was not far from Stonehenge. I asked the teachers, do you think I should write them? Do you think this is the correct address? And they said, you said you'd do it; you'd better do it. So I wrote the letter and sent it to the address I'd been given. A certain time passed. We started thinking about arrangements. This would entail quite a little something, you know. I would have to take a train to meet them when they arrived. I told the folks about it. When I told Doctor, he said, "I'd be glad to meet them with the car. Dad can bring them up to the hospital, and we'll all have lunch up there."

Well, to make a long story short, this was probably on a Saturday. On Wednesday, I looked out the window, and here was a tall, slender man, quite an impressive figure, walking ahead of his wife, with a cane and an umbrella and a bag in his hand, which happened to be one of those telescope bags. Now besides that, I had never met any lords and ladies. He was a lord but he didn't look a bit like what I thought a lord ought to. Lady Lodge had one of the sweetest faces you ever did see, and she had to caution Sir Oliver all the time, because he was always picking up something he shouldn't touch, or doing something he oughtn't to do, and I know she'd nudged him over again. He was one of those people, don't you know; when he got inside there were so many things that interested him. He had quite a charming manner, and an altogether pleasing voice.

And then Dad came, and he took Sir Oliver off our hands. Then it was easy! Lady Lodge followed me about. I took her to her room. She asked if she might take a nap, and I said, "Of course; we'll have a nurse come over from the hospital who can help you with your things. We don't have ladies in waiting or anything like that." She said, "Neither do I." I thought maybe she wasn't used to dressing herself, so I said, "If you'd like help dressing, I'll help you." She thanked me and said, "All right, I will call you." Well, she kind of patted me on the head as if I were half grown, and told me, "You have lovely children." And I said, "Yes, I think so, too."

Well, they stayed, and then I learned that she was a good medium. Her boy came in over and over again. My folks listened to the messages, and after a little while the children came in when the messages were given, and once Jack said, "Do you have a picture of him? I'd like to look at him." Jack was about 12 years old. He said, "If you'd show me the picture, maybe I could see him too!" Then Jack reassured me, "Don't worry; he's perfectly safe; he's with his mother and father!"

So that's my story.

**JOHN #1** If I could add something, Mary. Sir Oliver Lodge may have been forgotten by the majority of people today, even in England, but he was extremely famous in his time. He conducted a demonstration of radio based wireless telegraphy a whole year before Marconi started demonstrating his system. Only recently has full credit been given to

Lodge's patent, which was plagiarized by Marconi, who employed him as a consultant.

**MIRIAM WILLIS**  Lodge wrote more than 40 books about the Afterlife, relativity, and electromagnetic theory. As a Christian Spiritualist, he wrote that the resurrection in the Bible referred to Christ's etheric body becoming visible to his disciples after the crucifixion.

## CHAPTER SEVEN
## INVISIBLES, POWER STATIONS, BANDS, HIERARCHIES AND ANGELS

### 21 Stations of Invisible Helpers

**MARGARET**   We see on the chart, on our map of the Subplane/1$^{st}$ Plateau of Heaven, that 21 Power Stations of Invisible Helpers circle the Earth. It looks like those Power Stations are very close together. Could there be more than 21?

**MARY**   Let's say this: Between Heaven and Earth there are 21 Power Stations that I know about. As far as going farther than that, I do not know. But I know that all of the vibratory action that man goes through between life and death, he is empowered through those 21 Stations.

**MARGARET**   Are they closer to one part of the globe than to another part?

**MARY**   Peggy, to me, there's no measurement. Over there, I see something and I come back here. I'm not an artist, but I draw it; then someone who is an artist does a better job. It's a case of never forgetting what you see. And I don't believe that any one of you, when the door from the Channel opens into that world and you get a glimpse, will ever forget it.

**PATTI**   Then these Power Stations work not only for people who've passed beyond, but also for living people who reside here on Earth too?

**MARY**   They work all the time in both worlds. They are Power Stations that enable us to travel from one plane to another at night. I have often likened those first ones to a cable car. In going up, when going onto the 1$^{st}$ and 2$^{nd}$ Planes and beyond, they seem to lock. They go just so far, and they seem to lock.

**CONNIE SMITH**   It doesn't seem to me it would be possible for the 21 Stations to be in only one particular part of the world, because when people pass out, they die in all different areas of the globe; the power would just have to be everywhere where people are.

**JEANNE**  Do the 21 Power Stations of Invisible Helpers surround Earth completely, or just part of it?

**MARY**  No; just where the arc comes, as you see in the chart.

**JEANNE**  What's on the other side of the arc?

**MARY**  Hades/ Hell, Purgatory, the Magnetic Field – the regions down below.

**MIRIAM WILLIS**  Mary's talking about levels or vibration. You're talking about encircling the earth in its orbit, aren't you?

**JEANNE**  Yes, around the whole globe.

**MIRIAM WILLIS**  And we're talking of the vibration in depth, of Hades, Purgatory and the Magnetic Field being below.

**ESTHER BARNES**  Could you explain a bit more of our nearest contact to this whole thing, to the 21 Power Stations of the Invisible Helpers? If we need help, how can we approach the Helpers?

**MARY**  Those Power Stations are manned by Invisible Helpers, and that is 24 hours of our lives around the clock. Anytime I need an Invisible Helper I would say, for instance, "Bob needs you, he's had an accident, please go to him." There would be three invisibles that would go to Bob; they would come back and tell me the facts. It would take a little time to accomplish it, but the Invisible Helpers are the ones who work in all sorts of disaster areas. Invisible Helpers are serving God continuously.

**ANDREW**  I read that when an Invisible Helper goes to help someone, many times they take on the form of the person's concept of somebody holy - if they were Catholic, it could be the form of the Virgin Mary.

**MARY**  That's true. They would not shock you in any way. All kinds of people can call on them. To go about this, I would simply pray to God that the Invisible Helpers would help me anytime I was at a loss to know what to do for myself. But I would go the whole limit for myself before I would call for anyone, because our intelligence is supposed to help us do that. I do feel there's a lot people could do for themselves if they just were told how to do it. We're supposed to learn how to do it and tell another person who doesn't know. As far as the call to the Invisible Helpers, you would get a response.

**LOLA** I was privileged one time to hear a story Miriam told about Invisible Helpers who came to her aid here on Earth, and I wondered if anyone in the class had heard it too. It concerned an automobile and the changing of a tire in a snow storm back East. I think this is an opportune time to tell it.

**MIRIAM WILLIS** I was traveling with a friend, driving from Maine to New Jersey. We started about 4 in the afternoon. A snowstorm came, and just after dark we had a flat. We struggled to put this tire on. We both prayed very earnestly for help because we couldn't get the tire on. There seemed to be no one nearby. And then, out of nowhere, coming along the highway presently was a man, storm boots on, wearing an overcoat and fedora. He came around the side of the car on which we were struggling and asked, "Could I help you?" We said, "Oh thank you so much." In no time at all, he put the tire on. For some reason or other I went around, probably watching to see if any traffic was coming. When I came back to thank him, he was gone. We saw no car and could find no man. There was not a trace. My friend and I stood and looked at each other. But the tire was on the car. I had always thought he was one of the Earth Brothers who had the power to come out of the body and materialize. It was this kind of an Invisible Helper. I don't know if I am right thinking that.

**MARY** Let us be sure it was that way.

**PATTI** Why did this happen one time and not another? Like the man who was protected and somebody else not.

**MIRIAM WILLIS** May I tell a quickie that will illustrate this? It's about two children. They had nothing to do with each other. One little girl fell off a very high roof. She was not in the least hurt. She landed on the ground very gently. Her grandmother rushed to her and asked, "Are you hurt?" The little girl replied, "No, Grandma ... didn't you see? My guardian angel took me around the waist and set me down." Now, in

Detroit my three year old niece was hit by a car. She wasn't saved. She was a little girl, too. So we don't know the answer.

**MARY**   We can't answer that at all. I could name at least five cases where heavy equipment dropped from cranes and men were not injured. I lived for twenty years at an emergency hospital and you can't imagine the things I learned from what came in there. I had to believe in miracles, that people were intended to live, that it wasn't their time. Otherwise you couldn't think why.

**GENE**   Could it be that the life span was over, like for Miriam's niece, that she was only intended to live those three years?

**MARY**   I rest on the old statement: I am not God and I cannot answer questions like that. But my belief is, yes. These children that come and stay such a short time, many times are sent to teach those who have them, love.

**GENE**   In the case of the girl falling and being saved where she said her guardian angel saved her, would that be the case of an Invisible Helper?

**MARY**   It's within the law.

**GENE**   People think of miracles as contradiction to law. You mean a higher law when you say miracle?

**MARY**   Yes, we're talking of higher law. Always, there has been a time when people have spoken of miracles. Miracles are seemingly wonders at the time. Most miracles can be explained if you can accept development of the human soul, if you can accept man's belonging to God; if you can think of creative energy flowing through the human being and raising the vibratory rate of his intelligence to where he can see a vision so that it penetrates the consciousness. Miracles can be explained that way.

The Master walked the path of the unbelievers. Those people treading it, none of them truly believed until they experienced a miracle. But miracles were not just for the time of Christ and his disciples. Miracles are for today, only you must have faith in things like that to experience them. And think of the miracle of life itself. Think of the sights we have.

We are almost stunned sometimes, with the awe that comes up before us. We're asked, when we start the study of the planes, to so balance our three bodies that we think alike in all three. And therefore, we're so cleansed that spirit can speak through. And you get to the place where you know that God has answered.

**GERTRUDE**   Can you describe the Invisible Helpers? Who are they, and how did they get to be what they are?

**MIRIAM WILLIS**   They're high souls who've been trained, who inhabit this area as a resting place of refortification of their powers to minister to Earth in disaster, to help with healing in particular instances; to add to the happiness of people, to bless people and to support those in need in many ways. Having ministered to Earth, they can come back to the 21 stations and be replenished again and find an infilling of power so that they are able to stay nearer to the Earth for a longer period of time than they would otherwise.

**MARY**   Invisible Helpers have had Earth experience; they've lived here, they have graduated from Earth. They come to help in fire, flood, plane crashes and the like. I think history is just written full of being helped from the Other Side of life at times of disaster.

**ANDREW**   There must be thousands upon thousands of these Invisible Helpers, because so many people need their help.

**MARY**   There are all different groups that work as Invisible Helpers. Our class works with the Hierarchy of St. John. Healers work with the Hierarchy of St. Luke. A high guide might be what you asked for. Say that you were going to bring something forward to Earth that would be a redemptive force for many people. You might be spoken to by one from the 300$^{th}$ Plane. I would call him a high guide if he came through with a message that you could prove. Your sponsor would bring him, or a teacher might bring him. He would be surrounded with seven invisibles at least. People speak of high guides. I would say when they can prove themselves to be high guides, they are high guides.

**GENE**   Are the teachers masters?

**MARY**   I believe that's semantics. I usually call them teachers, and there are many teachers. Masters, yes, masters over certain areas of consciousness, masters that have achieved a wealth of information and are able to control conditions.

**MARGARET** If those in the Hierarchy of St. Luke are meant to do healing, what of the Hierarchy of St. John, which we're aligned with, supposed to do?

**MARY** We're supposed to be teachers.

**MARGARET** So many in our group have healing powers.

**MARY** If we have healing power, we can incorporate it as a mother heals a child. We don't have to belong to a group to use healing power. God at times moves very close to the man on the street to help someone. That's the Good Samaritan. If a person really takes up healing, I would say if you follow St. Luke, if you people become expert in this, you'll know a great deal I do not know. Because everyone attracts to themselves the thing that's best for them to know. One can work in more than one band - there isn't the separateness there that there is here.

**GERTRUDE** You speak of the power of the Hierarchy. Is it always healing power?

**MARY** I don't believe that there's any power that comes from that world that doesn't have the healing force, because it's a higher power than we can use commonly. It's the power of prayer. We can use that. And if we intensify it even in our thinking, think what it can do for us.

**ANDREW** Is the Hierarchy always available to us?

**MARY** Always. Those I know are in 12-hour service, 12 hours on duty. They're trained; all are under bands that train in the same way.

**HANK** Question regarding the 21 Stations. I'm not quite clear how those 21 Stations work. I understand how they function for the Invisible Helpers, but how do they work for us?

**MARY** Let's say this: I couldn't raise from one area to another over there were it not for the 21 Stations. And that's your answer. It supplies the power for the movement wherein we are raised from one plane to another.

**ESTHER ESTABROOK**   I have in my notes something about the helpers, that the 21 Power Stations help at the time of death, that they alert our loved ones we're going over.

**MARY**   Yes, they do.

**MARGARET**   Whenever we seek help, does it always go through the 21 Power Stations?

**MARY**   I wouldn't say that. If I were a $4^{th}$ Plane person, I'd go to the $4^{th}$ Plane for it. If I were $5^{th}$ or $6^{th}$, I'd go there. Because the teachers there are intimate with your life and they know what you need. In the transition of death, the 21 Power Stations take care of people going over who generally don't know anything about these teachings.

### Angels and Sponsors

**CONNIE**   In the meditation tonight, it seemed to me there was a complete canopy of angels. It looked like the whole room was covered with these angels. Angels seem always to be poised in beauty.

**MARY**   A good many of you have quietly mentioned to me seeing angels. They often come in an embankment. When we have been building so much power, the love creates that picture for us. We use this room for worship. What I love more than anything else, when the angels come they bank the children in front of them, those beautiful faces. And it doesn't last long. Glad you saw it, Connie.

I often saw the angels here, and then I would say to myself afterwards, I wonder if anyone else saw that? Then one by one, people would come and tell me, Mary, I believe I saw a bank of angels. And I said, well, they came as a cloud of witnesses tonight. I believe that's what they are, and that's the communion of souls. I believe it's sent as an inducement to us to further our faith and our belief in the invisible world, or shall I say, the real world. Having to live in the shadow, we came out for the moment in the great light of understanding.

**MARY JEAN COPE**  I read an article that said something about the real battle was not man against man but powers and principalities. Was this referring to angels?

**MARY**  I believe we could say that, yes.

**LOLA**  Didn't St. Paul say that?

**BERNARD**  "For our wrestling is not against flesh and blood; but against principalities and power, against the rulers of the world of this darkness, against the spirits of wickedness in the high places. Therefore take unto you the armor of God that you may be able to resist in the evil day, and to stand in all things perfect. Stand therefore, having your loins girt about with truth, and having on the breastplate of justice, and your feet shod with the preparation of the gospel of peace in the high places or heavenly places. That is to say, in the air, the lowest of the celestial regions; in which God permits these wicked spirits or fallen angels to wander. In all things taking the shield of faith, wherewith you may be able to extinguish all the fiery darts of the most wicked one. And take unto you the helmet of salvation and the sword of the Spirit, which is the word of God."

**ESTHER BARNES**  Mary, would you speak of the Order of Angels?

**MARY**  We're told that they never have lived on Earth. They were the stillborns, and they were those that were trained just in the spirit. And they have the great power of flight and carrying the message. Coming to Earth, they come in greet numbers. You can go into any of the temples and around the organs, before the great voice speaks to us in the temple, you will see them banked at night.

**WOODIE**  Is it possible some of us don't see the angels, but we feel their presence?

**MARY**  We have five senses and we're enveloped with our spiritual senses as well as our physical ones. I would have confidence when someone tells us they've felt the presence of angels. If I didn't see it myself, I would still believe that they were right.

**JEANNE**  Mary, what does it mean when you say the angels were stillborn?

**MARY**  They didn't breathe the breath of life or live on Earth. They returned to the kingdom of angels.

**RUTH**  When one sees spirit figures around a person, would those be angels? I didn't know what to call them, so I called them "spirit figures."

**MARY**  I think what you've said will do very nicely. It explains what it is.

**PATTI**  Could you speak further on the guardian angel? Does everyone have one throughout their life?

**MARY**  Everyone has one upon being born; all throughout human life that guardian angel will be aware of that person. To my knowledge there is one guardian angel to a person. They are with us for life. To know one's guardian, to be aware of it and give appreciation of love is a wonderful gift to them. They have chosen to be this.

**LENORE**  Does one have to be of a certain development to know one's guardian angel?

**MARY**  From the 4th Plane on you can recognize your guardian angel's guardianship. The guardian angel stands by the body at night when you're out.

**MARGARET**  I remember hearing that Miriam would thank her guardian angel for guarding the body while she was out of it.

**MIRIAM WILLIS**  Mary knows who guards the body each of us while we're out.

**CONNIE**  My understanding is that the guardian angel is not there always, that he or she is only there when needed.

**GLENN**  We can ask for them, ask them for help. But you don't have to call your guardian angel. If you're in dire need, your guardian angel knows about it and can come to your aid.

**MARY**  That's right.

**PATTI**  There are also ministering angels.

**ESTHER ESTABROOK**  We know everyone has a guardian angel, and we also have a sponsor. Could you say something about the sponsor?

**MARY**  We're supposed to have had chosen for us a sponsor who was not a parent or a relative, but a teacher who sponsored us into the world. And at times of disaster or any time that influence can be felt, we feel the presence of that person. And then, as you develop, you meet that person who has guided you. Other people call them guides. I call them sponsors because that is the act when your soul enters into life, that sponsor makes the remark that he/she takes this soul for guidance. As far as my knowledge goes, it's supposed to be something that holds a soul to the belief in God or another life, and that it is one world without end. And truly, "amen" came from that, being a complete world. In Old Egypt, "amen" was used in their language; it was used in almost every language that I have been able to decipher.

**MARILYN**  In our night work, when you take us to the Other Side, I saw a teacher with silver hair, wearing a gown. I kept pursuing it, wanting to know more, and then I got the name Andahl. Then, maybe a week later, I got in writing that he was my guide.

**MARY**  Let's take that in prayer, and don't be impatient; it may take a little time, but you'll get something that will prove it.

**BILL ESTABROOK**  Regarding the sponsor, I think you once said your sponsor is like your director. And that masters and teachers are both masculine and feminine.

**MARY**  In the days of Atlantis, many women were spiritually developed beyond men. Men had the power to put it down in writing.

**DALE COPE**  I have a two-fold question about sponsors. I was wondering if the sponsors are an interchangeable term for the guardian angel, or if that is entirely different?

**MARY**  No, that's what they were called. They're different.

**DALE**   And the second question: you spoke earlier about the fact that God was closer to us than our hands and feet. Are these sponsors or guardian angels a form that God takes in being close to us?

**MARY**   They are from God, these sponsors and guardian angels. But I wasn't thinking of a personal God; I was thinking of Creative Energy as it flows from that Creative Being. I can only think of it as a Being. I have never pictured God as a man. My mind wouldn't incorporate an individual with so much Creative Energy. But as near as I've ever been able to think of God is the love that I bore my Earth father. He's the Father up in Heaven, and he was close to us as children. We can think of God as a great rose of energy, every petal of which has energy going out from it. The Hindu speaks of God as a lotus, or the mother of God as the lotus. Anyway, it's a fragrance, the energy of God's love that probably would not convince a scientific mind. We have no way of directing something that we cannot see, the same way of getting a picture of it, is that not true? To go inside ourselves and form a picture, we have to take something from this world with us, do we not? I've had to go and see these things and come back and give English language, and the censorium of my soul love had to dip into it and ask what was that picture? And I ask to go and see the thing again and again before I ever dare repeat it. But you see, where a great many people have come into this truth and each one in turn has proven it for themselves, that's given me a great deal more courage to believe what I saw.

### The Christis Band

**HANK**   Someone said they saw Christ and had a conversion. Do you believe that person really saw Christ?

**MARY**   I wouldn't dare doubt that another person saw Christ, because I think it's possible. I just haven't had that experience myself.

**BILL ESTABROOK**   Didn't you say there are many in the Christis Band that look like him? And would you speak on the Christis Band, what it is, what they are?

**MARY**   They're a band of invisibles, and I don't want to influence you on the looks of the Christ, but those in the Christis Band all look so alike.

At times in temples you will see one of them, one or two of the Christis Band. They speak. One night the music was unusually beautiful and these two men in simple robes walked down this long aisle. Behind them were all the colors you could imagine. Soft bells were ringing. I asked what Band that was. They said, the Christis Band. That was about 35 or 40 years ago and I've never forgotten it. You see them many times in a temple or going out. Theirs is a type of worship. They must be at the top where the need is so great that they have to almost seek those higher souls for an understanding. I was praying the other night that the Christis Band would take our war question before the world becomes so involved that it can't get out of it.

They are the ones, it's said through teachers, that have held this prayer for many hours. So you see, they're not on the level, even with the Christ, but they have been trained in that way. They prayed for hours that World War I would cease. At the same time, small bands all over the Earth, brothers, were also praying for that war to end. Wars stop for a time; but until man can cease warring within himself, we cannot stop wars. There's a great sheet over there that hangs like a banner. That's one of the things that's still there. It's been there since the First World War times.

**MIRIAM WILLIS** If I may add a bit to that: On the chart, you'll find the Christis Band located in the area above the Healing Waters, but they go on up, way up in the planes. The Christis Band is comprised of those who've found soul development over many different paths of searching, and found that the standard of ideals and brotherly love as taught by Jesus the Christ are the highest to be followed.

**MARY** So we find that the Christis Band is comprised of such souls from many different nationalities and schools of thought who have joined this serving band and grown to become so like the Lord Christ, so closely do they follow his selfless love principle, that they appear like him.

**MIRIAM ALBPLANALT** I've heard that often people think they've seen Jesus when in truth they've seen somone from the Christis Band who emulates his life and teaching so closely that they look like him.

**MARGARET** Are there specific requirements to enter this band?

**MIRIAM WILLIS** The qualifications of the Christis Band are desirelessness, selfless dedication, prayer and service, concentration, love, devotion, loyalty and sacrifice, all principles of the Christ.

**MARY** Members of this band tie into Earth with their spiritual power and relay their forces out on whatever mission they're on to help the sick, the suffering and those in need. There's a great spiritual light shining from the Earth, a result of the many dedicated souls devoted to the Christ Principle in service.

**DORIS** Would you ever see one of the Christis Band on the Earth? We went to the Holy Sepulcher Temple in Jerusalem and this man came in. He was so like Christ that it stopped us in our tracks. He was the living image, the concept of Christ.

**LOLA** What would Christ look like to you?

**DORIS** I should explain it was the glory about this man, the light around his face. Our guide said he came from the other side of the Jordan. And he was light rather than dark complexioned.

**MIRIAM ALBPLANALP** There are some very blonde people in that part of the world with great soft brown eyes. They're not as dark as they're depicted.

**DORIS** Would there be a symbolic picture of the Christ that has been built by people worshiping, people believing? Like thought forms that people see when they pray that makes them think they've seen the Christ?

**MARY** It would be a lovely thing if it were so. We have seen the great statues and pictures of the Christ. The suffering one is the popular one we've seen, the man of sorrows. I've never believed he was a man of sorrows. I believe he brought love and happiness to the world. He knew why he came, he knew what was going to happen, and he was prepared for it.

**GEORGE** Mary, you've told us you're not an artist. But assuming you could, if you were to paint the Christ, how would you depict him?

**MARY**  Were I to paint the Christ I would paint him as a happy human being, a lover of children, a lover of people. He made the yokes easy in his father's shop – that's one of the things in the ancient documents.

**GEORGE**  The documents you've translated?

**MARY**  Yes. He made yokes for oxen different from anyone else's, because he took sharp knives and made them smooth, so smooth that they would not in any way rub on the animals' skin. That's in the ancient documents as I read them. And that is likened to the feeling I have of the Christ and his nature.

**LORNA LANE**  Over there, have you ever encountered someone like Moses or John the Baptist? Do you know where they are? Do you know where Christ is?

**MARY**  No. I don't know where they are. I've often wondered about that. I have never seen the Christ. The only thing I can say is that I hear a great voice. We assume that where that voice speaks, it's the voice of the Christ speaking through the temples. It's a melodious voice. We hear the voice but do not see the speaker. I have yearned to see the speaker whose voice I hear. I'd be afraid to declare I had, because out of longing we can make quite a little. That's all I can say.

## CHAPTER EIGHT
## BABYLAND AND CHILDREN'S LAND

**JOANNE**  I see that the Children's Sleep World is located on the 1st Plateau/Subplane, and I understand there's also a Children's Land somewhere for children who pass on, who reside there in the daytime.

**MIRIAM WILLIS**  Two areas, the Children's Land and Babyland, are located on a plane we will investigate later, the 3rd Plane. But perhaps Mary would like us to talk about the subject now, since Joanne has raised it.

**MARY**  Children who pass on stay in Children's Land on the 3rd Plane, until they're able to be moved into homes to be educated, to be given all the power of becoming fine adults. They have opportunities for growth the same as the life that they would have had here. After they leave Children's Land, they're placed in the many homes over there where people want children.

**MARY WERTI**  Is that what the island is for on the right hand side of the chart?

**MARY**  Yes.

**JOANNE**  What about the very young – newborns, infants?

**MARY**  For those who pass on so early, there's Babyland, also on the 3rd Plane. Infants and toddlers would stay in Babyland until the age of two.

**JUNE**  I don't know where the rest of you were last night, but I was in large place where there were a great many small babies in baskets.

**MARY**  You went to Babyland. It was a delight. Quite a number of us went along. I had the pleasure of going with my own mother. They were happy to show us the sweet, beautiful babies. If there is any place in the heaven world that is enticing to a grandmother ... those babies cradled in flower-like bassinets ... every imagination that could be put upon beauty has been created for those little ones. It's a place of pure contentment, and you leave wishing that everything on Earth could be like that.

**LENORE**  If they leave Babyland at age two, how old are they when they leave Children's Land?

**MARY**  At seven, the child is ready to be placed in homes that want children. After a child reaches the age of responsibility, he or she can be corrected very quickly, if he or she did the wrong thing. The nature that they were born with is still within them, and they express it there. Understand, if a child is five years old, that's a spunky, naughty little child. Because we're the same people over there that we are here. We don't become angels because we leave this world.

**CONNIE**  What happens after the age of 7?

**MARY**  After that, they go to special schools where they're trained till they're 14. They're taught in as many ways as they are taught here.

**HANK**  And of course, I assume they receive the equivalent of high school, college, and further than that if they wish, as they grow to adulthood.

**VIOLET**  I was thinking about a child I knew who passed on. She was in the children's realm, ready to get out of Children's Land. I was wondering about her growth to adulthood over there. This child had shown a particular artistic promise during her short life on Earth. I wondered if her artistic talents would be trained or encouraged over there?

**MARY**  There are different orders and schools that take our children, and they are trained for whatever particular talents the children exhibit.

**LENORE**  How do these children behave over there?

**MARY**  The children have their play times, they pinch each other and act very normal, they have rest times, they have their schooling, and they're happy. There is no unhappiness in Children's Land. That is something I can tell you that I believe with my whole soul, because I've visited there many times. They have correction there the same as in our world, only not severe. If a child acts up, somehow or other they find themselves standing all alone somewhere. They're moved by the motivation of spirit off by themselves, and they don't like that. A voice may speak to them and say, don't do that again, and they learn the lesson.

**PATTI** We learn that adults go over in different degrees of enlightenment, that some of them are discontented and unhappy about being over there and they go to much lower planes. Is it the same for little children?

**MARY** No. They haven't reached that age of hostility.

**SANDRA** When children have gone over in shock, suffered in an accident or something like that, or if they're longing for their people on Earth, don't those who take care of them put them to sleep as a way of administering to their grief?

**MARY** They're taken to a certain portion of Restland, where the child is given what you might say is a sedative, or a fruit to eat. There's the influence of whoever is caring for the child, but the child will sleep. When the child awakes, he has forgotten to a degree. Many times they take children back to Earth to see their mother and father. The child wants it, and is satisfied. When he comes back again, the child may not remember entirely. If the child is seven years old, they quickly let that child know it will be some time before mother and father come over, and that they are in this new world and will have to stay there. They accept it and go away contented.

**JEANNE** If children die, say they die the same time their parents do, and their parents also go over, what happens then?

**MARY** Their parents would take them, they would keep the child and raise it. And the child goes back for their training into the Children's Land every day, same as we send our children to school.

**ESTHER BARNES** So Children's Land and Babyland are mostly for children whose parents are still on Earth, but Children's Land is also a part time place for children who are living together with their parents in the Afterlife

**MARY**  That's right.

**ESTHER ESTABROOK**  Do they remain children?

**MARY**  Oh no. We would say that a 19 year old girl would, say, be 13. There is usually five to six years difference in their age over there. For instance, say that a child died at birth and now would be 25 years old. But over there, that person would not be more than 20, because it has to have a combined experience of the life that it missed on Earth, along with the spiritual training that it gets, to come of age.

**MIRIAM WILLIS**  Those who've lived in that realm, when they reach age thirty-five, have had wonderful training; they have mastered languages; they know the world below and they know the heavens above.

**ANDREW**  What's the point of their mastering languages if there's no need of language over there? I mean, everything is by intuitive vibration, everyone communicates without need of speaking any particular language, as I understand it. If you speak English but don't speak Italian, for instance, you can understand perfectly someone whose native language is Italian who speaks no English, simply by communicating through vibration.

**MIRIAM WILLIS**  The language training over there is mental, intellectual, a preparation for a future life on Earth, advancing one's thinking abilities and talents; it's a discipline for the mind. Is that not so, Mary?

**MARY**  Yes, and there are other forms of training the children receive which enrich them both for over there and in preparation for a future life here. Some people choose musical or artistic training, some want to advance in scientific or mathematical knowledge and abilities.

**ANDREW**  Would a person who was a poor math student in their Earth life have an opportunity to become perfected in math over there if they wanted to?

**MARY**  Yes indeed. I know people who resisted algebra as students on Earth, who realize they had a mental block and want to overcome it by mastering it over there.

**LOLA**   I would think this kind of training would make a person more proficient in their next life on Earth. It would help them learn things quicker, be better students next time around.

**ESTHER BARNES**   I see the Children's Sleep World is located on the Subplane. This is where our Earth children go when they sleep at night, isn't that so?

**MIRIAM WILLIS**   Yes, it is.

**MARY**   Mothers of children who've passed into the Heaven World by death often go there to greet and comfort themselves and their little ones. This visitation can bring solace to both mother and child.

**LOLA**   While it's tragic to lose a child, it's heartwarming to think it's possible to connect with that soul on the Other Side.

**MARY**   Now I'm going to confess something to you. You remember I released this little great-grandson, Stevie, who was so precious to me. Time after time I was asked, would you like to see him? Among my relatives over there are those who would take me, who would arrange it for me. My husband, Dr. Weddell, would ask me if I wanted to go and see Stevie. I always said no, I don't think I'm ready. Both my husband and my mother had told me that Stevie was a very contented child. But I just didn't want to risk it.

This week, I saw Stevie for the first time. I didn't speak to him. I went with quite a number of people over there who love him. I saw that child. He was walking along holding my father's hand, swinging – the same animated little fellow. I came back a much wiser and happier great-grandmother.

**JANE**   But you never spoke to him? He didn't know you were there?

**MARY**   I couldn't bring myself to talk to him. I thought I might fasten something upon that child that might draw him back to us. I've been with family over there lately, and I thought, God in his good time will take care of this. I told other people to be patient and thought to see if I had any patience myself. It was quite a test for me, but I did learn patience waiting. I saw Stevie as he is. I thought he was a fine looking child. I always thought him a lovely child. I loved his mind. Another thing: one person who loved little Stevie was Frank Crandell's wife, Ruth, who as most of you know, was in these classes and has been on the Other Side for several months now. Ruth always loved Stevie when both of them were here in the physical.

Well, Ruth said, "If you're going to see Stevie, may I go along?" I said, "Ruth, you know more than I do about it." Now I had gone to see other people's children, I had gone to see other peoples' fathers and mothers. But this was my own. I had never asked to go to see a child for anyone; they had always come to me. What a strange thing, I never dreamed I was going to say a thing like that. I hadn't realized I hadn't asked to see my parents; they came to me. These are some of the things that are very simple, out of my own experience. Well, that was my experience this past week.

Stevie has grown. He was always a very considerate child, and he had always had happiness, he didn't know anything but that. I don't believe, knowing the Other World as I do, that it's quite right for me to talk to Stevie yet. I must continue to wait. I want to say thanks that Ruth left me and went to Stevie and said hello, Stevie.

**EMILY** Can you tell us more about the things that go on in the Children's Land?

**MARY** As I stood there viewing Children's Land and the beauty of it, it is rolling country. I've never seen such beautiful lambs in my life, lambs that play over that sward. The children roll downhill. They play like normal children, although there seems to be not quite the roughness. I saw one little boy push another boy down, then pick him up. They do one thing I thought was quite remarkable. The helpers will bring the younger boys and give the older ones a chance to care for them, helping them grow up. It may be they needed to grow a bit in consciousness, looking after the little ones. It's the way our mothers do in the home.

If anyone had asked me, in God's world did I think that the simplicity of a child's life would be the bedtime story and all the musical ditties I heard when I first used to go over there, I would at have said, oh no, the child would have to be taught spirituality. So I've grown in my years, going to Babyland and Children's Land.

**DIANA**  There's a period when a child can't live outside of the mother's womb, and the child might be dead when it's born. If a child is dead when it's born, is there a life in there?

**MARY**  You're asking a question I can't clearly answer. I know there's a plateau of consciousness where children who have developed to birth ... say it has lived the full 9 months and is born but passes out after birth, if it has breathed the breath of life, now I know that much; before that I don't know. I know if it lives after that, the child is trained, that there is definite training for children of that kind.

**LOLA**  Do you think that before a child is born, the breath of life is in him, and he knows his mother?

**MARY**  From the teachers who've talked to me about it, from what I do believe, I think that at four months, if life is there, the soul of the child visits. It rests and gets acquainted with the mother. If there is love there, it comes often. If there isn't love there, the child becomes accustomed to coming and eventually the soul is conscious that it is going to be born again. These are deep subjects so we won't get into them. We might even offend somebody.

**VIOLET**  Are the children on the Children's Plane often taken to some of these temples where the other children gather?

**MARY**  The children who live on that plane go there. Yes, they're quite familiar with them.

**VIOLET**  There were several children in the Temple of Holiness one night when we visited. We saw them there.

**MARY**  Yes, but you know, we usually go to Children's Land to see them. Children belong there until they become of age in that world.

**LU ANN**  If a mother was going to give birth, would she know who she was going to get?

**MARY**  No, I wouldn't think so. I've known mothers who went to the hospital to give birth, who, if they believed in reincarnation, thought of someone they had loved in another life. They would call for that person to come back. I didn't know the person they wanted, or whether that person actually came to them as their newborn. They had a lovely baby; that's all I knew.

# CHAPTER NINE
# HOW MARY RECEIVED ENLIGHTENED TEACHINGS

**GEORGE** I wonder if you'd like to tell some of the new people how this teaching was revealed to you, at what age, and so forth.

**MARY** Well, thank you for wanting to know. I had studied music most of my life; I had a large extended family – husband, children, mother, father, siblings, cousins, aunts, uncles, nieces, nephews. My husband was a physician and surgeon. I'd had a concert career. Mine was what you might call the background of a happy and successful life. At 30, I had pneumonia, following which I had a staph infection. I fully expected to get well soon; I didn't think there was anything that would keep me from healing aright. I lay there in a beautiful room, sunshine, everything I could need. I had never thought I would ever be placed in a spot where I couldn't get up and get over it. Those who loved me were doing for me. I had no power in the world to relieve them of that.

The Mayos as well as a number of surgeons were out for a convention. Invited doctors had come from Germany and Bermuda and two or three other places that were singular and remarkable. One cardiologist said my problem was a heart condition, which it wasn't, and the elder one of the Mayo brothers, Charles Mayo, said, "This girl will never walk again." And he added, "I can prove it." One by one they came, sterilized their needles and poked different parts of my feet. It's called a "bobinsky reflex maneuver." There was no reaction. The next time I tried to raise myself in my chair I fell down on my knees. And that continued. For one year I was in bed, carried to the piano once a day. I got frailer because of no exercise. I had massage; I had everything a person could. And at last they said there wouldn't be very much chance that I not only wouldn't walk, but I wouldn't live any great length of time.

I asked my husband, "George, do you think I'll ever walk again?" He said, "I know you will." I asked, "How do you know I will?" He said, "Because I dream of nothing else but seeing you walk." And I began to have that dream myself. There was no feeling; I was eternally trying to find out if there was any feeling up to the knees, but there was none. And then I would dream I was walking. There were large bay windows in this room. When the sun got to a certain place, it always came into the room with a blast of light.

And one day I dreamed that I just felt I was moving; I was sound asleep. I felt I might be out of my body. I woke up, and I was at the window seat by that bay window, stretched out. I just stretched out on this velvet pad that was on the window seat, curled up and stayed there in the sun. It occurred to me somewhere in my mind, "You'd better get back to bed." That was all I could think of. Next thing I knew, I was in the bed. I woke and I thought, "That didn't happen to me. It's just my imagining." That happened over and over. The children would come home from school and always come up to see if I was all right. Then one day about 4:30 the nephew we were raising came up to the door, and I was over at the window. And the poor little fellow began to cry.

Someone asked me, "Were you in a trance?" I couldn't say; I only knew I walked. So then Father came up, and he very quietly asked, "Well, Mary, how are you?" By that time I was back on the bed. I have no idea of how to explain how I got there, but I was back on the bed. And I told my father, "I'm all right, Dad. Do you know, I think I'll walk again."

The biggest tears rolled down Father's face, and he said, "If God gave you the power to walk again, I'll be the happiest father on Earth." And then, because there was that emotion between us, we couldn't go on with it, or I think I would have told him then that I was perfectly sure I was walking that afternoon. Well, one night there was a fire, so I thought I would go over to the windows and see if I could see any light, as naturally as if I had never had the leg trouble.

I was over there, standing by the windows, and my husband came in. So he just picks me up, swings me over on the bed, and says, "Let's talk. Do you know how often you've done this?" I said, "No, but quite a number of times." He asked, "Tell me how you feel when you're walking." I said, "Strong and oh, so happy." He said, "Mary, you believe that you will walk again, don't you?" "I never doubted it." He said, "And I haven't either. But who was I, a man of my age, to contradict all the famous surgeons who said you wouldn't walk again?"

Then gradually, I'd get up at night and twice a day I'd have these walks. After about thirteen months, as these muscles were worked on by doctors, I became truly active. It took some time, I suppose fifteen months before I could walk across a floor and come back. But I was very strong in my shoulders and arms and I could play piano and the organ three to four hours a day. I was strong enough for that, and I had the old-fashioned pipe organ.

I think if I were not a grateful person I would not be here tonight. And out of it all came both the Color Course and the Planes Course. Because when I was at my lowest ebb, a voice said, "There are many things you're going to do, and the plan we have for you will mean you can help other people. I said right away, "My voice?" And they said, "No, you're going into the Music of Color." Well, color meant a great deal to me. But how could I make color music? They said they would teach me. So one teacher would come and stay with me maybe twenty minutes, then disappear, and in another hour somebody else would come. I took down reams and reams of instruction. My husband was just as interested as anyone could possibly be. And the family thought, well, if she never walks again, this is a wonderful new interest.

Out of that came many things. A doctor and his wife came to call through Dr. Weddell, who was always bringing people home to tea. We had tea upstairs in my room. This doctor asked me, "What do you do with your time?" I said, "I find it doesn't pass as fast as I'd like it to." He asked, "Have you ever thought of taking up Sanskrit? You know, it's a dead language." He asked me whether I'd had Latin and Greek. I said, yes, and Italian, thinking I'd had Italian for singing, and French, as we always do. He asked his wife, "Do we still have the Sanskrit books?" She said yes. He asked me, "May we come again tomorrow, have tea with you and show you our Sanskrit books?" Well, Sanskrit is what gave me the power to go in and help on the Scrolls, because Sanskrit is what led me to Early Hebrew and Aramaic.

**VIOLET**   Mary means her work on the Dead Sea Scrolls, which are written in Hebrew and Aramaic.

**GEORGE**   Did the teachers from the Other Side always come at the same time of day? Did you see them? Or hear them?

**MARY**   At first I heard them. They would tell me who they were, and seemingly the picture was reflected on my mind. But where they took me to the classes in the temples on the Other Side at night, I brought pictures of the temples back. One teacher might give me Planes one day, and the next day I'd get Color from someone else. They just gave it as my course is!

**GEORGE**  Did they come to you only when you were alone?

**MARY**  At first, yes, but Doctor used to hear them afterwards. At one point he came in accidentally.

**GEORGE**  Were you startled or afraid?

**MARY**  No, I was never afraid of the Other World.

**GERTRUDE**  Mary, you started to say Dr. Weddell came in accidentally.

**MARY**  Yes, and they told him to come in and take a seat, so he did. He was just as happy as he could be to be admitted, and they said, we know you have been very much interested in all of this science ... they always called it science. He said, "I'm not only interested, but I am so grateful for the restoration of my wife. You have helped her. Will you help me with other things?" And they did help him.

I will tell you now that he was very much blessed, because he lived and had hospitals during two wars, and he was young the first time. There were the big shipyards, and they were taking the spruce out from logging camps and the hospital at Camp Lewis, where he was head surgeon, a young man 35 years old. And the cases that came in were pitiful, because the men were not in any way alerted to what they were going to when they went up to log in the woods; they were not equipped, bodily, physically, or mentally for handling what they were given to do. And so, maybe a logging train would come down the mountain, and a lot of boys would be on top of it or a log boom would get away as they were reaching for logs. There were fires. All of that was pretty hard on Doctor. In the last war he worked entirely too hard. He saw 64 patients the day he passed—with heart trouble. They were short of doctors. The Army had taken so many.

At his passing, I was awfully sorry for myself, but I ultimately got to the place where I looked back and could say it was time for him to graduate.

You have to go on in order to know life as it really is. He's never far away, and I'd like you to get to the place where those that you love are as close as he is to me. Love is an invisible tie that never severs itself from the one loved and God. So Love is eternal.

**GEORGE**  I gather you have visitations from your husband?

**MARY**  Yes indeed, as many people in this class also do.

**JOHN #1**  May I ask: I know the five fans that are used in the color classes. Are there many more fans in the Temple of Fans?

**MARY**  Well, we should have six fans. We've never been able to graduate to the six fans. But it would be twelve in all, because of the harmonics of those fans. You know, if I give you color music, if we write color music, we will go into harmonics. The next fan would be the harmonics.

**MIRIAM WILLIS**  Of the basic six fans plus the harmonics, this would make 144 basic spiritual colors.

**SYLVIA**  And then we also have the extended rays.

**HELEN VON GEHR**  Would you have had all this if you had not had that time of enforced rest?

**MARY**  I don't know. I had enforced rest two other years of my life. The last time I did very well because I had many things that I could do and re-do. I had tuberculosis twice.

**HELEN VON GEHR.**  Were you more receptive because of this enforced rest?

**MARY**  I was down to bedrock. I'd accept most anything. You haven't any idea what a life that was to look forward to each day.

**GEORGE**  Mary, did any of the teachers ever tell you why you'd been chosen?

**MARY**  I never asked. You ask, George. Maybe they'll tell you.

# CHAPTER TEN
## NIGHTS IN THE HEAVENLIES - TRAVEL, TEACHING, TESTS

**EVA** Mary, I'd be interested to know how you came about taking people over at night to the Heaven World with you.

**MARY** Well, you have to work a long time before you're even allowed to do it, and then, at first you don't know who's going with you.

**EVA** I mean you, personally. How did you get started?

**MARY** I'm telling you, dear. I was probably in the work twenty years before I did it, and then because I seemingly had some talent which they could use, I was told I could take people with me. I would pray and think of their names. And then I would feel that when I gave myself in prayer, I knew I was going over. You know you're going to sleep, don't you?

**GEORGE** How do you begin? What's the procedure you use?

**MARY** You arrange yourself comfortably, but you just don't know when that instant is. I seemed to be alerted; I had to wait a minute for other people. That's all I can say. You know the English language doesn't accommodate to tell you these sensations that were so outside. It's like a lost horizon to me. I look back, and—how did I do it? But I do know that that was about the first time.

I was really inexperienced, but I seemed to be held. It's as if it's a mechanical belt flowing in light from here to there. That's about all I could tell you. It seems broad to stand on. It seems to be something that you never lift your hands from, this "carrier" that you're on. And you stand very steadfast and you feel that you're pinioned. But it's like the flight of a bird, and you go very quickly. I dislike riding escalators. I seem to have some sort of a fear of it. I don't know. So I just simply say, I don't mind walking up, or should we take an elevator? There's something in going out of the body that, while it's a simple thing, you know how you hate to release. For instance, when we're taking ether, the anesthetic, you know just that moment before it goes into effect you'd "rather not." That's the only way I can say that could possibly explain, but I have taken an anesthetic, and I know it's very like that. But that's as it was at first. Now I'm quite used to it, and I don't think about it anymore.

**ESTHER ESTABROOK**  I'm trying to form a picture in my mind of our going over with you. Unlike many in the class, I've never brought a recall of this through.

**MARY**  Each person puts their hands on the shoulders ahead of them, and that ties you. Now if you were to speak during that time, you'd find yourself flat on your bed, because you come back just that quickly. And you know, if you're doing this work, you know what has happened. You've spoken to somebody.

There's a great Sleep World, yes, but why lie like a log in that Sleep World when there are Temples of Learning that man has been invited to from down through the ages? Our great prophets talked of it, and in Revelation they describe all the temples that I've ever taken you to. And in our night training, we develop in a higher understanding, our understanding of humanity. Things that are of esthetic nature will appeal to us in a greater degree; we appreciate more than ever the love of people.

### Sleep Worlds: The Adult Sleep World and Earth Children's Sleep World

The Adult Sleep World and Earth's Children's Sleep World are two areas located on the left side of the map, the chart of the Subplane/1st Plateau. As we sleep, attenuated by our silver cord, our souls ascend to this area. Leaving the body through the chakra at the top of the head, the spiritual or soul body forms, and in this body, one ascends to the Sleep World. Located there are comfortable couches to rest on.

**MIRIAM WILLIS**  The Adult Earth Sleep World is located to the left of Restland on your charts. This place is spoken of in the Bible, where souls go while the physical body sleeps.

**GENE**  We're fortunate to have in you, Mary, a spiritual teacher who has the gift of being able to take people out at night to the heavenly realms. But suppose a person has no Earth teacher, yet wants to go to that world for teaching? Can a person go who has no Mary in their lives?

**MARY** In people without an Earth teacher, there often springs the desire to travel further, to live and grow in heavenly places of knowledge and soul development. If one desires to venture beyond the Sleep World where he would ordinarily go, he automatically emits an azure blue light that attracts a heavenly teacher to that soul seeking higher consciousness. That heavenly guide will offer to take that soul to the higher planes for learning. The soul will travel in the Master's power and begin his expansion in these planes of Heaven, returning to earth with perfect ease.

**ANDREW** Will they remember what they experienced?

**MARY** At first recollections may be almost imperceptible, but gradually this practice and the teaching in such sojourns promote further growth that the person will remember. Faithfulness in prayer and meditation in daily practice also stabilize and advance the soul's growth.

**MIRIAM ALBPLANALP** Question regarding quickening of mind in the adult Sleep World. Can a person who wants forgiveness meet another soul there for that purpose?

**MARY** Yes, but they would both have to desire it. If we're carrying too heavy a load, we can't expect of another person what they are incapable of doing.

**JEANNE** Do people who don't go to the heavenly planes but stay in the Sleep World, do they just lie there and sleep, or do they also have dreams?

**MARY** They dream, too, and the dreams are filtered to the intelligence of the dreamer. Sometimes their dreams will provoke them into finding someone who can solve their dream, and in so doing revealing to them that they have a soul that needs to progress.

**LOLA** How will they go about finding someone who can do that for them?

**MARY** Their desire is what the teacher sees, and the teacher answers the call.

**JEANNE**  If a person didn't have conscious knowledge about going to the Other Side at night, but they dreamed a lot, do you think they could be going out anyway?

**MARY**  I believe that they'd have to desire it. I don't think anyone ever goes that doesn't desire it. Years ago, I introduced someone to the Planes, thinking that I was right, knowing the person was so fine that I thought surely they should be in night work. And so I would take them and present them, but I always had to go to the Sleep World to get them. I don't have to do that to you people. You awaken at a call. So there's a difference there, you see? You have a desire. So through your imagination and your desire body, you answer a call.

**JEANNE**  Well, then what goes on in the Adult Sleep World for people who haven't come to the call yet?

**MARY**  They stay a certain number of hours in the Sleep World where they may have very active dreams. But they don't follow the dream or the vision. It really takes an outside force, does it not, in this world? It takes someone to arouse the imagination before you really believe in anything. We believe in something because our imagination has been aroused.

**JEANNE**  What about people who go to analysts and have their dreams interpreted? Are they working spiritually?

**MARY**  Oh, I think that every human being is able to interpret analytically if they really desire to do it and have a prayerful heart. I cannot develop you; I can tempt you, but it's God in you that does the developing.

**The Training Field in Night Work- "Grand Central Station" and Beyond**

Contact between Earth and the Heaven World is as early as Creation. It is the way to God for all mankind. The science of nighttime soul travel is mentioned in the Bible and by other religions as far back as 8000 B.C. This communication between the two worlds was an accepted reality for early Christians, who recognized that when human consciousness is focused on the inner planes in sleep, the liberated soul is free to commune with its own nature, partaking of the invisible world.

Out of the body night travel has been known and practiced for thousands of years; Indians, Tibetans, Persians, Egyptians, Greeks, Hebrews and others all embodied it in their teachings; it is a part of the inner teaching of all religions. All religious scriptures come from the same source, which is more ancient than we realize. Divine Wisdom tells us that the universe is the expression of a Conscious Life, whether we call it God, Yahweh, Jehovah, Universal Mind, the Universe, Mother Nature, or many other names. The Infinite Intelligence that transcends the power of human conception is beyond human thought or speculation. Every man has God within, a direct celestial ray from the Absolute One True Source.

When we contact that Other World every night as we sleep, our spiritual bodies are connected to our physical bodies by the spiritual cord, known as the silver cord. This cord is attenuated when you travel out of the body; it is extended during night work and severed only at death. This same silver cord is referred to in Scriptures (Ecclesiastes 12:6-7): "Or ever the silver cord be loosed ... then ... the spirit shall return unto God who gave it," and was known to exist from time immemorial.

As mentioned in the Introduction, Mary having mastered laws governing the ascent and descent of the soul between Heaven and Earth, summoned our spiritual bodies in sleep for night training, and helped us bring back recall of our experiences. Every person enters the rhythm according to the development of his soul.

**MIRIAM WILLIS**  You people might like to have me show how we go out at night. Look on the chart, see the Power Line, see Nature's Creative Energy. When we venture into the Heavens at night, we're taken in sprit by way of the Power Line, shown on the left side of the chart. The soul travels on the silver cord along Nature's Creative Energy to a gathering area on the 3rd Plane to then be taken to a higher plane for training.

**ANDREW**  This gathering place on the 3rd Plane is what Mary refers to as "Grand Central Station."

**MARGARET** And from "Grand Central Station," we branch out to the temples for our teaching and testing.

**MIRIAM WILLIS** That's right.

**ALMA** I was wondering about the position of the Power Line. It seems to go through all the Planes of Spirit – the central Plane?

**MARY** When we go as a band together, it reminds me very much of a cable car. There isn't any noise, but every once in a while, there's an impetus of movement of that power as we're going through to the Spirit World. And that's about all we do feel. It's a very steep ascent and very quickly done. That's what those Power Lines are. We know we're higher, in more power. I used to ride a cable car, so I've often thought of it in that way. It's hard to manufacture words that can describe something you've never seen.

**HANK** What about the River of Life? Isn't that a way to the Heavens?

**MIRIAM WILLIS** When one passes away in death, one goes through the River of Life. But when we go out at night, we don't go through that River.

**MARY** We would go that way only in death, the way every man goes in death.

**MIRIAM WILLIS** The Channel of Nature's Creative Energy to the right side of the diagram is our way of approach. It directs us toward transformation. In our training as developed people, we enter the Heaven World through the Channel of our Being, the Color Channel, which we call the "Keys to the Kingdom," which takes us to the Fount of Supply. And this is why we practice going through the Channel.

**MARGARET** The Fount of Supply is also on the map there, on the chart.

**MARY** In our nighttime travel, we travel on etheric lodestones, one behind the other, in a line. It's like an interminable glittering chain of vivid light composed of magnetic circles that are all looped together, one into another, which sweep around the realms of space like flowers in a ribbon of fire.

**CONNIE**  Those lodestones are pictured on the maps, too.

**MIRIAM WILLIS**  The lodestones are ice blue, a beautiful opaline blue.

**MARY**  It's the light of the lodestones that lift us as we go climbing through the planes, as we're carried along. Every so far, there will be lodestones. It makes me think of a cable. Every so far in cable cars, they lock, and that is as it seems when you go over a lodestone. It's a lift, and a lift and a lift. As you travel through the Heaven World, many times, if you're riding on this rail of light or this wide ray of light, you feel that lodestone as it's picking you up as you go on, as it's picking up the power to carry Earth beings who are in the Heaven World.

**LOLA**  You said the lodestones lift Earth people; they temporarily raise our vibration?

**MARY**  They furnish the creative energy for us to move. We're in another realm, and while our spirit bodies dwell there, we're in the spirit body. We are Earth people thinking Earth thoughts, being taught to live in these heavenly bodies for short periods of time.

**ANDREW**  And our first stop over there is "Grand Central Station."

**MARY**  We go very fast. As we're going up, each of us is holding our hand on the next person's shoulder. That Landing Field on the 3rd Plane where we stop briefly, to me, it's "Grand Central Station," because so many crowds of people are landing here, people from all over the world. Someone comes in and a number of people leave to go off with this group or that group. We wait our turn until we're told where to go next.

**PATTI**  When we go out at night, the silver cord remains attached. Can we see that?

**MARY**  We would not see our own, we would see the other person's.

**MIRIAM WILLIS**  The only way we can break the vibration is by speaking. Now, in each case, that silver cord is suspended from Earth to Heaven, and it is the Creative Energy going through us that keeps us on that ribbon of light that we're going to the other world with.

**YVONNE (VONNIE) BRANCHFLOWER** It seems I'm aware of what this Grand Central Station is like, and I've also been aware that there's a lot of quiet but very happy anticipating talk.

**MARY** That's when we go out from a temple. There's a spiritual gallery that runs around it, and after you're released from the vibratory activity that you stand in, then you can go out there and you can talk.

**HELEN MARSH** When anyone speaks of Grand Central Station, I receive a vision of a broad path, always a large building in back of me. I see temples. It's a wonderful feeling.

**MARY** Well, embrace it, because the temples will be given you, and the description of them will come through that vibratory rate of our thinking. In other words, we become accustomed to bringing things through, and after a little while it's always there for us.

**HANK** Why do you call the place we land at "Grand Central Station"?

**MARY** I have no other word. I don't carry with me a built in language; I've never been able to create a language that is descriptive enough for this work.

**GENE** When we go out at night, what are the bodies that go along with the soul? I know the physical body is left on the bed, but I wondered what are the bodies that clothe the spiritual soul that goes from us?

**MARY** We have light bodies in the spiritual body. So as a glove is to the hand, the physical body is to the mental and the spiritual body. When we go over permanently we take with us the mental and spiritual body. We have all of our memories, and we have all that we have lived in this life within our mind. We know the people we've been with. We are aware of all that has been placed in the fullness of our lives. Therefore, we're able to answer to what we've done right and what we've done wrong. As we're conscious living human beings on this Earth plane, when we go to the next world we take with us and present just what we are, not what we think we are. Worldly honors amount to very little unless they have contained within them a benefit to mankind, which many honors do contain. And justice is always there.

**JUNE** I'm a little confused about the difference between the Adult Sleep World and where we go at night with you, Mary, to the temples on the planes.

**MARY** All Earth's children go to the Sleep World. But most of you are so ready you hear the call and don't need to go to the Sleep World first. You're taken right away to the Planes for teaching in the Heaven World.

**GENE** But everybody in the world has some degree of spiritual experience at night?

**MARY** Everybody goes somewhere. If they're not in development, not in a teaching like ours, they go to the Sleep World. Going out and being taken out are very different.

**MARY JEAN** When we go on a night trip do we have an aura?

**MARY** Oh yes. We carry our aura with us, and it does a great deal of good because it's our spiritual balance. The aura is a spiritual balance of a physical body. It also contains all of the elements of the physical enlightenment that we go through.

**MARY JEAN** Well then, while we're on that trip, the body on the bed doesn't have an aura?

**MARY** It has the shadow of the aura.

**FRANK** Shadow, but no color?

**MARY** Oh yes, there is a color in it. Remember that it is as a hand in a glove; the spiritual body retains the aura, and it is as a hand in glove. And as the hand is taken out of the glove, and it glides on its way, it carries its own light, and the light is the aura. It surrounds the spiritual body. And on the bed, because the body is inanimate when you're lying very quietly and still, the aura hasn't as much of the radiance, as it has gone on.

**GLENN** Every year it seems there's new people come into the class, and I know they wonder how you take them over to the Other Side, Mary. They wonder if they should try to prepare themselves for it, and I'd like to tell them, no, don't do anything. Forget about it.

**MARY**  Yes. To go to sleep with a prayer on your lips is the kindest thing you can do. That's right, Glenn. I think just prayer—you ought to go to sleep with a prayer on your lips.

**WOODIE**  Then I can't say, "Mary, please take me along?"

**MARY**  I'd be very grateful to be recognized.

**GEORGE**  What has to happen to the individual before he becomes aware of going out with you? Some people bring back vivid recalls, while others don't remember very much, if anything.

**MARY**  You have to take it on faith for a while. Could you accept the fact that you go to temples at night? And then, after you've gone into the state of belief, you take a foundation of faith.

**VIOLET**  Even if you don't remember your night work, the essence of what you experience is impressing your soul silently, and will affect your Earth life in a profound way. Eventually, you will start to have recalls.

**MIRIAM WILLIS**  When one is taken out by a teacher and arrives on his plane of development, his soul is intensely awake and entirely conscious upon the spiritual plane. The individual sees, hears and senses the presence about him of those upon the spiritual plane who are waiting to receive him. As Mary has often told us, we hear these words: "This earthly life you live now is only an intermediate stage. For every one of you has lived before, so shall you live again. You have not seen the great architect of your life, nor do you completely understand his plan. But we, your teachers, know there is a plan. Accept it in faith. May you, as you look back to earth, see the stepping stones leading upward. May this be your creative prayer."

### Training and Tests

**JUNE**  Can you tell me what the primary activities are in our night work, once we get over to the Heavenly Planes each night? What do we do over there?

**MARGARET** May I respond? The activities we experience in the Heaven World are geared to our own level of understanding, with the goal of increasing that understanding so that we become more fully developed people. As a group, we attend inspiring ceremonies and gatherings led by highly evolved teachers, many from the 100$^{th}$ and 200$^{th}$ Planes, in which we're imbued with greater wisdom, knowledge and love. We meet our heavenly guides, then branch out individually for guidance, to take spiritual tests and receive initiations and healings. In these private areas of personal growth and testing, we face self-correction, seeing our mistakes and clearing the subconscious, all of which enables us to live with greater wisdom in both worlds. We're storing our treasure in Heaven and preparing our future home for the transition called death, which isn't an extinction at all, but a welcoming into the fullness of the Afterlife. In the temples on the planes, we're imparted with heightened spiritual energy that carries over into our daily lives on Earth. The tests we're given there are later paralleled in tests in our lives in the physical world. Another activity many of us engage in over there is training with Invisible Helpers, to learn to better serve God's Kingdom. And one of the most enjoyable of our activities there is visiting with our departed loved ones.

**JUNE** In our night work, we go through tests, and we come back with the awareness that there's something we have to clear. So we're clearing things we would be held responsible for later on, when we become discarnate?

**MARY** Yes, you're cleaning house for the next life. There are many little hidden things in us that need to be recognized and cleared out. They crop up again and again.

**GENE** I'm interested in the kind of tests we have over there.

**MARY** You're given fire, water and air tests. The fire tests deal with physical purification; water tests purify the emotional body; and the mental body is cleaned in air tests. There is specific testing and development in each temple, and afterwards, there will always be an Earth test to match.

**MIRIAM WILLIS**  In our night work, our consciousness is given healing, so we'll do better the next time a test occurs.

**CONNIE**  When we take those air tests at night, we go across giant chasms. Are we frightened?

**MARY**  Very. Stark with fear.

**ESTHER ESTABROOK**  And we do these tests for balance?

**MARY**  It's a wonderful balancing to have faith enough to go to the other side of that chasm. To find your balance will give you a thrill that you've never had before.

**ROWENA**  I was thinking about the fire test, purifying the physical, and wondering if it isn't possible that the lower emotions of different kinds do descend into the physical and that's what has to be purified?

**MARY**  Umhm. You said it.

**ROWENA**  Thank you. Because one of the messages that I had that made such an impression on me is to purify our emotional selves as much as we can before the fire comes.

**MARY**  That's it. If we can just find our balance in living. We build in these classes here a web of faith and chemical substance that to me always seems like a silver net. It's as heavy as a fishnet. But it seemingly is linked by links; it's formed that way.

**MIRIAM ALBPLANALP**  I remember a recent fire test which brought this question to mind: does the fire test cleanse and purify the physical, and the water test, being liquid, the mental/emotional; and the air the spiritual?

**MARY**  That's right; that's very good. You've said it very plainly.

**MIRIAM ALBPLANALP**  The fire test is the type of test which would burn away and help purify the drossest material that we're made of, which would be the physical body, which would be on the corresponding wave length to that heaviest one of our three bodies?

The water test, being next lightest in fluidic and wave length content, would burn away and help cleanse the mental/emotional body of our being, and the air test, being of the highest vibratory rate and lightest material, would help cleanse and purify our spiritual body?

**MARY**  Thank you. That's well said.

**MIRIAM WILLIS**  Over that chasm is an air test where you're on the escalator of faith.

**MARY**  All through India, they expect to cross these great chasms or deep ravines using rope ladders. And quite a number of doctors who work over there have told me the sensation of stepping out on those ladders and keeping your balance. They're tied in squares of very strong hemp rope. And these doctors have told me that the bravest man turns white at the first few steps. Then they seem to get in the rhythm and the balance.

But also, before them and behind them go the natives. So that's keeping the balance. This one doctor said that at one time he wasn't on the ladder when it spilled, but natives were going over and one had a pet dog, a small dog. The dog jumped on the ladder and the rhythm of that dog upset the ladder and they all went down into this rushing water. And they're very much afraid of water when they're rushed into it. They'll go into any kind of ocean water and think nothing of it. But these rope bridges are a test even to the natives, let alone men who have not been on them before.

**MIRIAM WILLIS**  And man is blessed when he can accept these things.

**MARGARET**  Is it possible that we might go through certain tests that might appear harrowing?

**MARY**  If those are tests, you will know it, you'll be told they're tests.

**HELEN MARSH**  I remember going up so many steps to the top of a hill. Then I go out on a platform and there's no place to go. I never know how I get back. That has happened several times. Why would a person have an experience like that?

**RALPH**  I think many of us have had that same experience in testing.

**MIRIAM WILLIS**  I've gone to the very edge, and if I didn't look and step back, I would have stepped off into nothingness. That's when you've gone as far as you can go.

**EMILY**  I recall a great many experiences with water tests. These tests seem so profound.

**MARY**  A water test is a deep dream. Many times we're tested going through water, and again, many people have said to me, I know I went through water and I came out, but my clothing was dry. Water would be around you in some way. You might be struggling against a current or be out in the rain. Usually it makes you remember things you shouldn't forget. At night we're released from this subconscious that drags us down on Earth. In the temples we're released from the hold some things have on our minds.

**VONNIE**  Mary, how does one get over an intense fear of water? I feel like if I saw a water test approaching on the Other Side, I'd head the other way. What should I use to get over it?

**MARY**  Go with it; bathe in it; be thankful for it; know that you have been initiated into the depth of God's love and the waters of life have closed round about you. It is, you might say, a baptism of love. You know the direction when you come out. You know that there's something you're doing that's been washed away. Now you may not know it, but if you take that longing fully in your heart, the answer will come. God answers prayer. But I think that's very wonderful, because you're young in this particular teaching. Thank you for telling me.

**VONNIE**  Thank you for your advice.

**JEANNE**  When you're born, you come a reverse direction too, don't you, a reverse of the direction we go in death?

**MARY**  That's right.

**MARY JEAN**  At night when out of the encumbrance of the physical body, is it easier to experience spiritual awareness?

**MARY**  Yes. We're more sensitive when we shed our physical being, our body. Say we're in a Band and everybody is in a state of expectancy, we nearly always get our reward by getting something we expected. But we are also told that expectation could be fulfilled on Earth. We really are on Earth for a purpose. We're fortunate to have this training, but we shouldn't feel that our night work will take care of us, because our action here on Earth is the very important thing of our life.

**PATTI**  Sometimes I have dreams during afternoon naps. Do we ever go to the temples in the daytime?

**MARY**  If a person in the work has missed a night, it seems during naps you don't lie there idle. A teacher comes and gets you.

**EMILY**  I was wondering about dreams and visions. I have them, then I'll have periods where I don't receive much, and then it starts up again, very strong. I'll bring back recalls from our night work that way, and sometimes I'll receive something quite fascinating in the daytime, just as I'm nodding off, even catching a snooze watching the news on television, or something like that.

**MARY**  There are some people who dream a great deal during sleep time; there are people who dream very little and have vivid visions, even if they lie down in the daytime. In some of the greatest visions I've heard people tell about, they were sitting in a chair and dropped off to sleep.

**LENORE**  Would that be a spiritual vision dreamed?

**MARY**  Your dream might be a spiritual vision, and you'd be in the spiritual body.

**LINDA**  I was wondering, Mary. What do you usually wear in the temples when you go to the Other Side? Do you wear anything special? Do you wear something different each time?

**MARY**  Something is thrown around me, Linda. It's a color that goes with the people I'm working with or what we're trying to accomplish. Very recently I have had mostly rose, lavenders, or the color of inspiration. But you always put your keynote color on when you enter a temple.

**LINDA**  Whenever I think of the temples I always picture myself in the light blue. Do we wear our own clothing?

**MARY**  You're in your spiritual body and you have a loose, filmy robe that's quite dense. You pick it up and it's weightless, but you put it on and you feel the weight of it. So we do feel weight; we do have sensations and pleasure. We have great pleasure in tasting; we all are in higher spiritual senses. We see a beautiful scene and we enjoy it until tears come to our eyes. Now I do not know; there may be Planes higher than where I've been where that's not true. But God has provided a sense of education, shall I say, to the soul that goes over and keeps trying to move upward on the tiers of many Planes.

**DORIS**  When we gather at night, do you have to go and fetch each one of us?

**MARY**  No, no. We go over, we just come together, dear. And if one is late in getting over there they just naturally go to the Sleep World, and then a guardian angel or someone who is very much interested in you will go and bring you to the class. And it's almost as quick as thought that it happens.

**GENE**  About how long does our work go on over there?

**MARY**  I only have time by the way I live. I work there at night and I live here by day. My teachers and I have tried to use time to give you some concept. We work over there about 5 hours a night. We're in the Sleep World the rest of the time. If you're too tired to go along, you stay where you are. So it's about 5 hours that you're in the temples doing the work of developed people, going out with invisible helpers. Each night they start to work at 12 o'clock. Three hours in the temple and two hours for general work.

**MIRIAM WILLIS**  You know, our work in the temples at night, though we may not always consciously bring back our experiences, nevertheless has deep roots in the innermost being and does affect our whole life. Many times the reflected experience from a temple will manifest itself in a most surprising and practical test in the human life. Often you're looking for something spectacular, beautiful and wonderful, and when it doesn't come like that, we just don't recognize that God is training us.

**WOODIE**  So it's possible for a person that you've taken there at night not to realize it the next day?

**MARY**  Oh my! I should say! Sometimes they go a long time without realizing it. But they see the changes in their lives, and on that, they build faith. First, our belief has to be tested, and out of that belief you put faith there. On faith, we started from the time we were children. Now we add that element of faith to $4^{th}$ dimensional thinking, and know that if we've gone, it will be given to us.

**MIRIAM ALBPLANALP**  Do we ever cross paths with any of the other people? I mean, might we see other groups on the Other Side?

**MARY**  If we were going to the Temple of Worship, yes. They come up on another side. We would have one particular entrance, they would have another.

**MIRIAM WILLIS**  And you know we see other groups at Grand Central Station. When Mary takes us over, we're together as a class, hands on shoulders, moving up on that sort of escalator that glides very swiftly, and we arrive at "Grand Central Station." You wonder where the people all came from, the same as you would if you were in Grand Central in New York.

**PATTI**  Are the other people in Grand Central Station brought there by teachers who, like Mary Weddell, are in the physical body?

**MARY**  Yes, certainly. Grand Central is where all people who come in for work in the temples meet. It's a teeming mass of people, but they all seem so orderly. There's one in their midst that has the orders, and they follow the leader, all nationalities, all races, and we're just one in the midst of them all.

**MIRIAM ALBPLANALP**  Mary, speaking of the influences, isn't it true that the condition of consciousness in the soul affects the place it will find itself in; for instance, if one over there suddenly becomes angry, they'll automatically lower their vibrations and find themselves down.

**MARY**  They just naturally go down. Let's say the elevator takes them right down, and they disappear for a time until they become poised again, and then they can go back to where they were.

**MIRIAM WILLIS**  And if you become critical over there, you suddenly find yourself all alone, in isolation.

**MARGARET**  As I understand it, if we're awakened suddenly, we disappear from the group. Then sometimes we're back with the group.

**LORNA**  You say we're at work over there for five hours. We start out at midnight. Well, many mornings at 5 a.m., I have this sensation of landing on my bed with a big thud. I understand this is when I'm returning to my body.

**MIRIAM ALBPLANALP**  This problem will go away in time, once we get to the point where we're more balanced; then that no longer happens.

**ESTHER ESTABROOK**  On one of the Planes, is there a place where people can be taken to be healed of unhappy memories of their life?

**MARY**  For some ways up, we continue to have to have these places on each subsequent plane, and I'll tell you why. We have a great long life to review if we have lived here on Earth. Many times we go in and review a particular thing, and it makes us unhappy. So we ignore it, go into denial, we turn the page and look at something more cheerful. Each time they take us back to this Temple of Remembrance, we're forced to look that thing right in the face. After a while, it dawns on us that's our particular problem. It isn't erased, it's still on the board. Then we face it. That's what gives us the chance to go on in this climb, which is a weary climb.

**GRACE**  Do we record a lot of the things that are not to our benefit?

**MARY**  Those fields of justice are the most real and altruistic things you'll ever know. Man gets credit for things he doesn't dream he'd get credit for. I believe that as we develop, a greater part, more than half, is to our benefit. I believe we should be very proud of our record when life is done. The greatest accomplishment we can hand back to the Father is a life that's ready for eternity. Every night we give back something to the world. Night work tells you what you need to go on.

**SYLVIA**  Don't we actually place things in the temples there that remain? Then we bring with us a reflection or a feel of what we've left there, and there's a dynamic created between the two which assist the manifestation.

**MARY**  Yes, we've made manifest the creative energy we've been talking about in the channels we use there to recreate and send back to lay treasure in Heaven. It's a powerful thing. We don't know the creative energy that flows through until we really test it for ourselves.

**EMILY**  Are we correct that knowledge and wisdom are imparted in the temples, and that gaining these advanced states comes by lecture and by both group and personal instruction, and do we have a chance there to go and do likewise?

**MARY**  You go and do likewise. The important thing is practice. Our potential has to come through and we put it into practice. The mind has its dark spots. When development comes, we're rid of them. Then of course, we've seen what we do there and what we're asked to do here. We reflect it in our daily life. In a great many temples you'll find a repeated phase of development, something poignant that goes through these temples. You have a desire to know your way, your future. You'll probably go back in this particular area in another few years. Your night work will come through, you'll know what you do at night. You'll be able to record it yourself.

**GENE**  Mary, those of us who are in groups, not only this group but other groups who have night training, we're doing it purposely to develop ourselves, our souls. But how about those who seemingly have this ability naturally? Higher sense perception, as it's sometimes called. Evidently they don't know anything about ever having had any training at night or reason to have these abilities such as seeing the aura, etc., and yet they do have it, never having studied it or worked for it.

**MARY**  I know there are many people who do have it, as you say, Gene. Many people borrow through the natural imagination, and their pictures are so real they feel they can obtain the development. And there are those that are not willing to be tested along those lines, and there are those that work very hard whom it takes a long time to acquire what some other person acquires easily. I might say to someone, you're a natural; it'll come easy to you. And it will. And the person sitting beside them takes a long time. But this person is absorbing the right chemicals, and when the time is right, they will show great development. And the person who had read a great deal and especially the mystic teachings of the Far East, all that sort of thing, they are indoctrinated to a degree, and they have a natural ability to absorb more than the person who has never heard of anything.

**LOLA** What is the best starting approach to spiritual development?

**MARY** I've said this before, I'd like to say it again. Everything that I have in life, I started out by taking on faith. What I don't know I'm privileged to prove. You do see the adventure of life. It stays with us, going on and on. Because we know that within ourselves is that building thread of life, and it's one world without end, amen. I believe that's the reason it was given to the Lord to pray the prayer, to show us it is without end, it is one great world, and we are endowed with the privilege of so living that we find peace here and hereafter. It takes patience, but development comes.

**EVA** You made a statement a while ago that I may have misinterpreted, but you said we're especially privileged in relation to the Other Side, that we had experiences others never had, or something like that.

**MIRIAM WILLIS** Yes. We have the development.

**MARY** We have the development that we need for there and for here! You know, this is a two-way street, there and back. I've testified to the fact that no man is deprived of living in immortality now, if he can so live. Because the Master said, "Where I am, there shall ye be, also." And he has shown us the way. So we're privileged in living both there and here, as he did. His voice speaks in these temples. We know his voice, and we know the blessing, the reverberating tones of that voice, the sympathetic understanding are so great that you feel as if you've been given a blessing. We go in as a company, and we sit there in the quiet and wait. Eventually, a light envelops our aura, and he speaks. And we know, hearing that voice, that it truly is one world without end, and that we are living in eternity now.

**GENE**  We're fortunate to have you, Mary, to take us out at night. But for anybody who doesn't have an Earth teacher and wishes to go to the Planes, he can go there as well.

**MIRIAM WILLIS**  Yes, desire is the impetus. Desire will attract a heavenly teacher to take the person out for night work on the planes.

### The Akashic Records

**LOLA**  You were going to speak of the Book of Life, Mary.

**MARY**  In the Hall of Remembrance, we see this Book of Life. Our subconscious is a dark cave that has to be cleared of everything until the self revealing self becomes an open book to us. God has made such a far reaching and marvelous provision for this within, yes, but a provision that also registers elsewhere. It registers in eternity in the Lamb's Book of Life. It registers, if you want to use another term, in the Akashic Records. There's nothing lost in that land where the Great Creator has made everything perfect. The Book of Life records just this.

**MIRIAM WILLIS**  You know, when Jesus said that the Father cares for the sparrows, and there's not a hair of your head that isn't numbered – this is truer than we think. Everything that has affected the life deeply is registered there.

**MARY**  When the soul travels forth in night work, if we have earned the right and the time is right for us to go there, we're taken to the first Hall of Records, where we view our lives. You see the aggregate of the benefits and the results of failures and weaknesses. Everything that has deeply affected our life is registered in those records. The purpose of the records is simply that we may later, even though we've tried here to clear our subconscious, be able to see our record. This is an amazingly revealing thing. We see exactly what God's purpose for us was in this life, exactly what the plan of our life was meant to be.

**ESTHER ESTABROOK**  It takes a degree of spiritual power to be able to bring this back into the conscious mind, of course. How are these experiences brought to our conscious awareness?

**MIRIAM WILLIS**  Through dreams and visions, recall, building pictures, divine imagination. When we bring these things back, the power to do this is furnished.

**MARY**  Through the wisdom of those who have been endowed with great imagination, we find wonderful allegories of truth, all the trappings of imagination which intrigue in the story, and the narrative form clothes a truth. They sometimes hide a truth, and only discerning can discover it. The Bible is full of it. This is true of much great literature; the fables, the fairy tales are true of this. Allegorical writing is filled with it, much poetry is filled with it.

**HELEN FLATWED**  I notice on the chart it says "Vale of Records of the Last Life." Now is this something that you go through, or is it a consciousness that you receive?

**MARY**  It's something you go through, and from the experience there, your consciousness is heightened. You want to go into the Hall of Records. You want to see for yourself. One day, you turn to see a teacher, you follow this vibration, you see you're following a lighted ray. You go to wherever the teacher is, and you're told when you'll be able to go to the Hall of Records, at a certain time—they might say "after temple time tomorrow," "after you go to the Temple of Song tomorrow," and it is the next day.

**ANDREW**  I thought you couldn't reckon time over there.

**JOHN #1**  They have to have a way to designate an appointment.

**MARY**  We say it's time as we have here, but there certainly is a rhythm of day and night, lessons, learning, anything that lifts the soul. And then, you're permitted to go to the Hall of Records. And the first thing you see is the record of your life. This present life is the important life. This is the thing that you're enlightened upon almost immediately. It's the first privilege that's granted you. You go up there and you see yourself. If you've written a book, the book is there. If it was worth writing, it will be in your hands, and you'll see certain sections that have been blanked out because it wasn't truth; it was a delusion. Sympathetic understanding is one of the laws of spiritual attainment. And spiritual understanding means that we've lifted ourselves on wings of enlightenment and that is on that record there. That's just one of the little things that I can say. But you read what you've done in this Earth life. After you've been there a good while and proven yourself, you're allowed to know your past lives. The Akashic Records are open to you after you've attained the 4th Plane over there.

From the Hall of Records, you go to the Akashic Records, where you can read the records of your life; then you're privileged to read the record of your father's and mother's, usually mother first. Then on from there, you see why you've made two marriages instead of one. You've seen how you've paid a debt with the first marriage, and that you were just as wrong as the other person, but at least it righted itself in life. You go to a world of perfection, you stand there and ask, "Why did this happen to me?" They never tell you why. The teacher leaves, and before you know it, through the movement that is natural movement over there, you find yourself at one of these "why did I do it" tables, and the record of yourself and your life is there for you to scan.

**MIRIAM WILLIS** If you can look back on your lives and see that there was no anger, no jealousy, no distrust, you can wipe everything off the slate. Then, say this has happened to me to make me more of an understanding person, and perhaps I can help others. Sometimes we're given experiences of jealousy and misunderstanding just so that we're to have our eyes open, that we may grow in stature, and recognize how other people whom we see are walking too close to the edge of the abyss of misunderstanding.

**MARY** One can get over that edge so quickly! I have a feeling that if you believe you haven't wronged anyone, then God and you have an understanding. And if you feel you have ... now, there are many people who wouldn't stand for your coming and apologizing. They don't want your apology. Pride is the wall between you at that time. But the walls of Jericho broke down, so believe that someday that wall between you and another can be broken down.

If our hearts are pure and we still keep praying for the people who have misunderstood, look very closely at yourself, and say, was I dominating the situation? Did I in any way move too far into the territory of their thinking and cause them to resist me? The moment we build resistance in the mind of another person, we have created a difference between us. These things are registered in the subconscious according to the depth of impression. Great shocks, traumatic occurrences, behavior patterns, poor health patterns, fears, depressions are all registered in the subconscious. Everything that has deeply affected our life is registered in those records.

**GEORGE** You've mentioned imagination and divine imagination. Could you speak more about that?

**MARY** There's a point where imagination ceases and we enter into truth. Divine imagination is beyond our conscious mental imagination. It's linked to Christ consciousness and the development of our soul. It's a bridge to truth. This ray stems from the great creative source. We all recognize a great thing when it comes and we're looking for it. But visions are built on small glimpses. The glimpses or visions that you have in that other world are the things that keep you on the path. When we make pictures, our physical imagination meets eventually with divine imagination.

**MIRIAM WILLIS** The color of deep rose purple.

**MARY** Divine imagination is given to all mankind, especially to seekers on the path. In seeking, that treasure is ours; no one can take it away from us because it's hidden. When we make pictures, our physical imagination meets eventually with divine imagination. Therefore we must know that in seeking, that treasure is ours; it is ahead of us and we are preparing to keep it. We're becoming attuned, sensitive to the vibrations of refinement that helps us as seekers to become aware of wonders awaiting us through the Channel. Why were we given imagination? Every beautiful thing in the world that's ever been created had to touch the imagination. Then if it touched divine imagination, its creativity was that much more refined and delicate. You can see things through divine imagination, you can bring those things through. But you have to take something on faith. The reward of faith is to use oneself as proof, your own experience, not someone else's.

**DALE** I've become aware recently of how important imagination is. I used to be afraid of imagination and still am, so I've been trying to let my imagination go, and tonight during meditation I just said to myself, now let's imagine here. And I imagined that I could see one of the Teachers. I wonder if there's some explanation for what I feel I saw? I had a vision of a very large man with white wavy hair and white beard, very ruddy complexion. I couldn't figure out his actual garment, but he was holding in his hand a torch, something like the Statue of Liberty holds, and it was actually a flame coming out, but the flame which turned to smoke wasn't smoke but beautiful color. It seemed to change a little, but it seemed to flow all over the room, over all of us. And it seemed at times it was waving. Now was this my imagination, or...

**MARY**   I could show you a picture of it. I was given a book for my birthday, and on the frontispage, Lola Grube has that picture painted. You may see it. That is one of our teachers. Will you name it, Lola?

**LOLA**  Philo.

**MARY**  Philo. And he has worked with these groups many, many times.

**VIOLET**  Suppose you go over and your life is very filled with service for your people. Do you not carry over some of that sacrificial attitude enough so that it would still be with you?

**MARY**   Violet, the history of the lives that we've known have been people who have served, and God's world is just as filled with need for service as this world. There will be a place in the scheme of things for every one of us. After becoming acclimated, we go to the Akashic Records, and we see what has made us fail in our lives and what has benefitted us. And then life's problems are put out against this wall of light, and from there you are shown what you can do. Your mistakes cease to be.

**LOLA**  The sacrifice is a credit to us on the Other Side if it has been done in love.

**MARY**  That 's right.

**MARGARET**   It seems to me that karma must be important in the Akashic Records.

**GENE**  Yes, so many people would say, for instance, someone who had something happen to him, well, that's his karma.

**MARY**  No, no I don't say that at all. I don't teach what to do with your karma. I believe if you so live day by day, Gene, that karma is just a background, and you walk right away from it. By the time you're walking toward the Lord and doing your best to live, then karma is your background. We can't undo what has been. But we can walk away from it and have the pathway clean and bright, and the karma will take care of itself. Many people use it as a mask or a great excuse. "But how could I help myself; that's my karma!" You don't know that. You can't prove it. And I can't prove many things that I'm saying. But I have a solution for getting away from false ideas!

**ETHEL**  To explore it a little further, I was wondering if in past lives you may have had another name, and through recall you may recall other names that you've had. Wouldn't that be possible?

**MARY**  It would be possible, but I think the usability of them would be lacking here on Earth, because we were sent here to live this lifetime. And believe me, we have plenty to live up to. And it would only be to interest ourselves further in this to look back. For by the age 30, according to all the work that I've ever taken in Egyptology or Hindu work, or the record of the early Hebrews, after 30 or so years, if you've lived your life well in your first 30 years, your karma's behind you; you're making karma from then on.

**MIRIAM ALBPLANALP**  Presumably good karma!

**GERTRUDE**  You mean after the first 30 years everything we came here to do has been done?

**MARY**  The load should have been taken from your shoulders. So just dwell with the idea: I can't do anything about that past 30 years, they are behind me, but I have another 30 years or more ahead of me in which I'm going to accomplish everything.

**GERTRUDE**  Will we know whether or not we've accomplished that?

**MARY** I would take for granted that I had, if I had lived I decent, moral, upright life. I think then I would say to myself, I know I have. I have wronged no one willfully. Then you could say, ten years out of my life I have been an adult and I haven't gone into any life and disturbed it to the extent that I couldn't be forgiven.

**MIRIAM ALBPLANALP**   Supposing you have, but you've made recompense?

**GERTRUDE** Sometimes we're told that we have.

**MARY** Oh yes, you'll be told from the Other Side in your night training: now you've made that mistake before in other lives ... do not make it again! And it does impress you. And you may willfully start out to do something and reconsider.

**ANDREW** The gnawings of conscience, messages from the higher mind.

**ETHEL** You may be able to condense the timing, I understand.

**MARY** There's something that comes with us. I don't call it a load of karma. I think when a man or woman is 35 years old, karma is done for. You've got all you can do with karma. But you can build a new karma as a road to Heaven, to the Other World. But it's the recognition of the truth that there lies within you, whether you want to recognize it or not, it's right there, and it's a built-in condition. So open up and air it, and just see.

## CHAPTER ELEVEN
## RECALLS AND QUESTIONS

**RALPH**  Sometime between midnight and six o'clock this morning I had this vision of a huge cross. It was flat on the ground. It was paved ... smooth as a piece of glass. I was standing at a cross roads. And all of a sudden I started making figure eights, moving just like I was on wheels, but each of my arms would move out, make these figure eights.

**MARY**  Wouldn't you say that's two worlds? Figure eight is two worlds, is it not? And you must be at the union of two worlds. There must be a decision, a worldly decision, first, to start with. And it you were relieved of some of the worldly decisions you would have made time for the spiritual decision. Is that not true?

**RALPH**  Yes.

**MARY**  The figure eights would be that to me. The cross is the thing that we ever carry with us. Every man bears his cross. Every man IS a cross. And with the head lifted we become as Christ was on the cross. So every man bears his cross. And as he becomes enlightened his head is held higher. And he is a seeker. To become a seeker is something that imbues man with a God-like substance. He has so much to give. He is never hungry, because he receives. And as ye give, so shall ye receive.

**HELEN VON GEHR**  In the quiet time I asked for anything I could receive to give, and I had the vision of a teacher, like a monk, in brown robes. I couldn't see the aura, but there was an outline of stars around. He carried a lantern. I asked him why, and he said this was the light unto the path. So then I asked, "Where are you going? Where are you taking me?" And he said, "To the Temple of the Grail."

**MARY**  We go there.

**LOLA**  Mary, yesterday morning, as I woke up, I was repeating a long word. It was a word I had never heard before. I'll try to look it up to see if it exists. Were we given something like that? Is that why we're repeating something as we awaken? Is that testing?

**MARY** Oh, yes! Many times it's testing whether we bring things back or not. The simplest messages are training you to bring back what you need to bring back, for proof to yourself that you're developing the spiritual body.

**LOIS** Whenever in the past I realized I was leaving my body in a half awake, half asleep state, I get panicky and come back right away. A week ago I had an experience. I started to drift off to sleep and somebody was right there beside me by my bed. It frightened me, even though I knew it was nothing to be scared of. I'd start to drift off and the person would be there. I kept trying to call out, and my husband said you're dreaming, having a nightmare. But I wasn't. How can you get over this panic?

**MARY** I would get a drink of water first of all, then I would start in color. I would go to sleep in sunset. We have to trade that fear for faith before we can enter the Channel and really see. After you've once seen through that telescope into the other world, there's nothing but kindness. I'm not going to tell you not to fear, I'm going to say use faith. Robe yourself in purple.

**LOIS** When I was fully conscious I knew it was no one who would harm me.

**KATHY** The other night I felt I should go to my 8 year-old son. He was sitting up in bed and he said, "Mommy, someone keeps calling me. They keep saying my name. They say Rodney, Rodney, Rodney." He was afraid.

**MARY** I can't say what's best for Rodney, but I know what I'd do if a child of mine said that. I'd ask him, who would you know that would be calling you? At 8 years of age, one has quite a mind. I'd say if anyone loves me enough to call me in sleep, I wouldn't be afraid. Then I'd sing a lullaby. I would lie down beside him and cuddle him. I would never let a child accumulate fear of the other world in any way. Some teacher will work that out. Maybe that someone who was calling wanted to see your child while he was over in Sleepland. Then the child suddenly came back. That person may have called Rodney, Rodney, don't go back yet, or something like that. Anyway, it was real and your son heard the voice calling.

**ESTHER BARNES**  Last night I saw many people, adults, walking by me rapidly. They were dressed in clothes of about 100 years ago, but the curious thing about them was that the clothes and the people were pure light colors, as if they were all made of porcelain china. The pale colors ... is there a meaning?

**MARY**  Yes, in development. They were developed people and they had gone on into higher color. Once in awhile we meet up with bands of them in the temples.

**ESTHER BARNES**  Why would they be dressed that way?

**MARY**  It's an insignia. As we dress for the Order of St. John, they are in their insignia. The form of dress probably originated at that time. They've lived over there that long.

**SYLVIA**  Don't we get any new attire over there?

**MARY**  With that matchless material that is handed to us ... it's a web of something or other. Hold your hands up and you can clothe yourself in the most remarkable colors. It's outside certain temples. If you're in rapport with the work and in harmony with the temple, if you want a robe of rose, you put rose on; if you want purple, you put purple around you. But you can create your own robe and you stand in it. The moment we start to come back, you'd love to bring it back with you. One night, a girl next to me said, I'd love to have a robe made of tiger lily. She meant it, she loved those colors. She said, I've always loved tiger lilies and day lilies. She had a tiger lily on and a day lily with little flecks of pale yellow in it – both were strikingly beautiful. She was inflamed with the idea she loved something. You dramatize to a degree, you use that creative energy that is free to use.

One woman said to me, "I would just love to create a big doll like that beautiful child over there." The woman was instantly handed a doll. She held the doll for a short time and by the time she had walked ten steps the doll disappeared. It's a magic land in that we're not deprived of anything. The beauty and glory of it makes you discontented with Earth if you let yourself be.

**AVIS**   This vision I brought back from our night work seemed to be in two parts. There was a white temple on a rolling hill with a fountain before it, not a spraying fountain, but a pool of lovely clear water in a blue stone enclosure. Someone was standing there, wearing a deep blue robe with a rose-red lining. This person seemed to be offering the blue water in a crystal cup, and when I took it, suddenly I was going up steps, and the person turned into a shining vision with gold about him.

**MARY**   You visited the Temple of Truth, the first temple we attend as we start up these planes. The Temple of Truth goes all the way up through all the planes. You'll meet up with this temple no matter how far you go, and you'll come back to various dimensions of it according to the need of the truth you're endeavoring to understand.

**FRANK**   The first Temple of Truth we go to? Where is it?

**MIRIAM WILLIS**   The Temple rises at the top right of the Hierarchy.of St. John on the 1$^{st}$ Plateau/Subplane.

**MARY**   The substance of truth is revealed there. One is stripped of his opinions and prejudices, freed from the deception of outward appearance and limitations. He unfolds truth to the extent of his capacity.

**MIRIAM WILLIS**   The truth of each soul is revealed, if there's a wish to know.

**MARY**   As the vision nestles in the mind untouched by the things that sully or corrupt, man is stirred to the deep places within. A gulf lies between our goal, our dream and its fulfillment. As man emerges out of sleep, he knows that all things reveal themselves, if he has the courage not to deny in the darkness what he has seen in the light.

Then man is awakened. Think of waiting as a window opening on many landscapes. Think of waiting as a time of intense preparation for the next leg of the journey. At last comes a moment when forces can be realized and a new attack upon an old problem can be set in order. For many seekers, waiting is even more than this. In this time of becoming, the seeker gains balance. He also realizes he's developing creative power, forming a pattern of recollection in which there is called into focus the fragmentary values of life he has held in his consciousness.

**MIRIAM WILLIS**  All that becomes clarified and unified.

**HANK**  You mentioned the Pattern World, that is, I believe you referred to it in describing the location of the Accident Arena. I'd like more information on the Pattern World, what it does and how we're affected by it.

**MARY**  There's the world of creative force called the Pattern World, wherein are recorded accomplishments in science and the arts, available to all for edification in these areas of endeavor.

**MIRIAM WILLIS**  It lies just below the Temple of Truth on the Subplane.

**MARY**  The Pattern World is tremendous in size, as you can see on the map, on the chart. All things created by man are first conceived with the inspiration of God's creation. They're always first created in this Pattern World. Many artistic or scientifically inventive souls seek their inspiration in meditation or deep thought. They're often taken to this Pattern World at night to see their "creation" before it infiltrates from their soul into their mind. Most people of this type seek to be inspired and feel humbly conscious of inner visionary help.

**VIOLET**  And that great Pattern World over there has everything imaginable in it.

**MARY**  Indeed it has. I believe it's one of the greatest privileges in the world to go out in night work and go to the Pattern World and see what it holds for the future. In that Pattern World, you can see things through divine imagination. But you have to start with faith. As your faith increases, your dreams will come through, and you will understand them. The reward of faith is to use oneself as proof, your own experience, not someone else's.

**MARGARET**  Mary, I had a very clear recall from my night work this week of a series of tests, and it also seemed to be in the Pattern World. I wanted to know if in our night work on the Planes, we're tested in the Pattern World as well as getting new things from there?

**MARY**   No, it isn't a testing ground of faith. The tests come in the temples, through faith; through living the life of faith. But the Pattern World is a place of adventure and ongoing.

**MARGARET**   I had an experience of the Pattern World. I was told to watch a screen, because it seemed that anybody who watched that screen, anything they saw that they could use, it was there in their hands immediately. What I saw were new molds.

**MARY**   Oh yes. That you can get in the Pattern World. Yes, I agree.

**MARGARET**   And then on my way out I noticed some beautiful table settings and this and that and a new organ it was a three-cornered, sort of boomerang shaped affair, and I remembered thinking, oh I must remember how they do that!

**MARY**   Well, that's a good record of it; maybe you'll remember it and be able to use it.

**MIRIAM WILLIS**   One of the chief activities of the Planes is that of seeking. And one of the first things that struck my mind, before you get to the 1st Plane, is the Pattern World. You know, there has to be a spirit of seeking in the heart and soul to go to the Pattern World, to discover the great creative things that are displayed there. That was the first thing that really impressed itself deeply on my mind.

**LOLA**   In regard to the visions that come, the other night I asked if I might have a glimpse, so that I could really feel I knew them better, and in the morning I recalled enough to draw pictures of them.

**MARGARET**   Mary, last week I saw three extremely distinct, very small people standing in the open end of what looked like a huge cornucopia. I thought they were in a temple someplace and that was a special door, but I don't know!

**MARY**   Often when one is seeing through the Channel of their being, the figures are not always life size. The Channel often is like a telescope, smaller at one end. Sometimes people liken it to a morning glory or a trumpet. It is as though at the end of that you see the small figure.

**GENE**... Mary, you mentioned there are people in this class ... Violet, Margaret, Esther Barnes and Sylvia are four you mentioned ...you said these people have brought descriptions of night work and temples ahead of when we go there. My question is how do they get them before they've been there?

**MARY** Receptivity in prophecy. Some people are given to prophecy. They can predict ahead what they're going to see. It's in the visionary nature of some people to look ahead. Visions are a part of the visionary nature. These are things that are natural things, these are the growing pains of development, learning to wait and apply, learning to take what little bits we have, and patch up. Or thinking as it were.

**LINDA** Is it true that when we get over there that we can have any kind of a robe or clothing that we want? Do we just wish it, then have it?

**MARY** If you were going along with the Order, with the Hierarchy of St. John, and you were working with them, you would wear what they have. Otherwise, the choice would be yours.

**LOLA** I was wondering also if we would always have our personal colors? Would that be part of our robe?

**MARY** Yes. Many of my people will find themselves putting colors together that belong to their personal plume. They may wear colors that maybe others wouldn't wear. One lady the other night had five scarves on. She made a beautiful blouse of them.

**IDA** Mary, the other night, I took an astral flight, you might call it. There was someone who might have been a teacher in front of me. At first I thought I was in a small plane, and then I realized I was standing upright. They took me high above what seemed like a sand colored crater, or a no-colored crater. Over on one side were little structures like where cave dwellers would live. There was no way to get out of this. Then we went higher and over, above again. There was no vegetation down there. I was wondering where I was.

**MARY** You were probably crossing over beyond Hades, because the thing that is taken from Hades is the green of the Earth and the beauty;

it's just not there.

**BARBARA**  Mary, as most of the class knows, I have a sister on the Other Side. Every once in a while I'll see her in a dream. Recently, someone else saw her beside me and said she looked sad, not happy. I thought perhaps the sadness was concern over things that we were going through?

**MARY**  I'd say so. Jo comes into your vibration; you reflect that condition upon her. I don't believe she has anything to be sad about; she's well adjusted. She was happy before she left.

**HELEN FLATWED**  What is it when you get part of a sentence left in your mind and that's all you remember? I could still hear the words when I woke up. This was on Tuesday morning.

**MARY**  Had you thought, when you were very quiet, of taking your pen and seeing if they would add to the sentence?

**HELEN FLATWED**  I do have my meditation time when words come into my mind and I pull them down - I haven't tried for a long time.

**MARY**  Finish the sentence, it might be interesting.

**JANE**  I come back and don't bring much physical description of the temples, but I do bring back what I think may be the night work. One night I had what was to me a wonderful experience. I seemed to be working in a hospital. I especially remember I was taken to the bedside of several people who were preparing to go into the next life. They were happy about it. In one case, there was an elderly man whose sons were standing around his bed. He was making arrangements for them for after he passed on. He tried to comfort them. He said, "To think, maybe tomorrow or the next day I'll be with Mother." This left me with a joyous feeling. Then I was back in a group. I was telling the others how people were happy when they lived and how happy it can be when one is glad to be going over. They all smiled at me like of course, we knew that all the time. I felt it was a real experience.

**MARY**  It was a real experience. Keep track of them when they come. Because there will be a day when you will be very glad. If you have these experiences, write them down. That is your night work. You have gone some place you were directed to go, and you have touched immortality with the realization of eternity. A memory like that is very consoling at the end of one's days. And I'm sure they would smile at you because they've all have the same experience.

**JOHN #1**  Is there a place outside the temples where we can speak personally to the teachers?

**MARY**  Yes. Just a prayerful desire - a teacher will be standing there, waiting for you. If a person is really desirous to know, no stone is ever given for bread. They give the bread of life, and it's freely given. And the corridors of the temples of Heaven are filled with many teachers who are so willing to walk along with you and just talk about the things you need to know.

**ROWENA**  This morning, returning from our night work, I saw a patch of color. I don't know if it was one color or looking through two colors, light or yellow-green, I'm not sure, but it gave a cast to the underlying color which seemed to be opalescent, like fish scales, very small detail, and very beautiful like mother-of-pearl, yet not really mother-of-pearl because mother of pearl is too gross; this was very fine.

**MARY**  Over there, big books will have iridescent, almost metallic covers, it seems. As you open this Book of Life, your own Book of Life, many times you exclaim at the beauty of this outside cover. You open it up, and there you are revealed to yourself. I think that's what it was. That's what you saw with that patch.

**EMILY**  I experienced a dream or a vision recently of being with my teacher whom I loved very dearly. He unrolled a long scroll and showed me ... I don't know whether it was my past, my good deeds, my bad deeds or what it was. I wondered if that was the Hall of Records.

**MARY**  Yes. Things are scroll-wise there.

**LOLA**  I was awakened about four or four-thirty, and I had to get up and write. I saw a curtain. I realized that my mother, who is on the Other Side, and I were in a long court behind a castle-like building, where we discovered many beautiful ceramic tiles of different sizes, colors and shapes, which were partly embedded in soil. We saw several large ones with a sort of a basin-like center which would make very interesting bird baths for our yard. And then I was looking at this long stretch of waterway; a curtain of vapor was being let down to make the light, or the sun, intense light – less intense and more beautiful and restful to our vision. And I thought of many times when in these various readings and visions there has been this curtain, and I wondered what the significance was.

**MARY**   It's probably something that you've seen in a past life, the memory form has come through to you, and you've been given it again. Look for it over there. See if you can find it. It would be pictured there. As we go back in the Akashic Records there are some things that have been discovered, uncovered, as it were.

**HELEN VON GEHR**   This comes to mind, a vision I had of a lady one night. Her dress was colorless. I can't remember what she was doing, but all of a sudden that dress changed to the most brilliant blue.

**MARY**   You must have given her something that caused her spiritual body to come forth, and she demonstrated it in her spiritual body. Sometimes when we're with our loved ones over there and they come to us, they feel they must appear so we can recognize them in a dress they used to wear. In no time at all, a teacher will come along, and they just breathe a word, and they change to the kind of colors they deserve on that side. Say they've been over there for twenty years, we're breathless at the beauty that's displayed. I've had lots of experiences meeting with people who've been over there who have become beautified. Through Color you exerted the emotions to the extent that you could see yourself in true reality, and through that reality which is God's world, we could match our traits of character to the higher laws of the Heaven World. In so doing we raise the vibrations of our body. Eventually, by matching our vibrations in our night work to the heavenly vibrations, the chemistry of our bodies is changed; our minds grow, and we have a dimension in thinking that we have never had before.

**HELEN FLATWED**   I never bring anything back, but I hear a voice. The other morning the voice brought me a name and numbers that I thought sounded like a telephone number. But I can't locate it.

**MARY** That's part of your development.

**HELEN FLATWED** It was a Czechoslovakian name, Marachek, and the number was 311-8516. I kept saying this over and over in my mind as I wakened, as I came to consciousness.

**MIRIAM WILLIS** Maybe she's a relay station.

**MARY** Yes, that's true, too. There are many things that we could say, but we're just using our judgment when we say it. It could be, as Miriam said, a relay station. They're using your spiritual self to help someone in healing or in work that you need to do for your own development. And it might be that you were called to help that person. We call them relay stations when we're approached that way. But you do have the voice of prophecy; it's very close to you. There are about four people in this room that have that. And they could do a great deal of good. Ruth Thomas is one who has the Voice of Prophecy, but she's too timid to try to use it.

**MIRIAM WILLIS** Mary, there was a time when Edith and I used to get things like that. Do you remember the direction you gave us was to repeat the name and number and send it on a prayer, that you're being used as a tie-in, for that to be sent on for someone else to get.

**HANK** What exactly are the activities of God's People's Prayer Plateau on the Subplane?

**MARY** It's where our spoken prayers ascend, are empowered, and sent on to their destination.

**GENE** I have a question about religion over there. How is that manifested, when there are so many sects on Earth and so many people are set in one or another?

**MARY** There are no sects in Heaven, but everything is recognized. So if I wanted to be a Methodist, I could be a Methodist. If that's something that satisfies my soul, I stay with Methodism until I can go on. It's evolution, the evolution of the human soul. There's no rigidity. In Heaven we are one people. We naturally go to the thing that attracts us, and nothing stops us. If there's a Baptist minister and someone has said

I used to be a Baptist; would you want to come over and hear him, and we go there, that's fine. There's no force, no evangelism, no in fighting and arguing. But if you meet up with a minister whose church you attended on Earth, you'd attend his church over there because you would want to be back to the familiar treadways of life.

**MIRIAM WILLIS**  Until you're ready to accept a more universal teaching.

# CHAPTER TWELVE
# COLOR, THE CHANNEL AND KEYNOTES

### Color as a Measure of Spirituality

Mary saw her Color teaching as stepping stones to self realization, knowledge, spiritual development, cosmic attunement, and understanding of how to apply universal law in everyday life, so that we might realize our rightful inheritance to live compassionate lives in wisdom, health, harmony, abundance, peace and love, which is our inheritance. She believed that the knowledge of long-lost color meanings revealed to her and her development in the skill of using color were harmonious with what Jesus taught his disciples, when he took them apart and taught them many things.

The over one hundred, fully tested etheric color rays Mary brought through from the Other Side consist of five spiritual arcs of color with 12 rays each: the Spiritual Arc of Green – "Growth;" the Spiritual Arc of Red – "Metamorphosis;" the Spiritual Arc of Blue – "Training of the Ego;" the Spiritual Arc of Yellow – "Illumination;" the Spiritual Arc of Purple – "Spiritual Balance;" and four psychological arcs (green, red, blue and yellow) of 12 rays each, plus a number of Extended Rays. Many of these colors are not simply shades, hues or tints, but combinations of colors containing midrays, or colors described as either "streaked with", "tipped with," "touched with," "dirtied with," "overlaid with," "underlaid with," "with side shadings," "striated," "striped," or "swirling."

There is no quick way to describe Mary's elaborate and elegant color teaching. It's a lifetime study, a matchless spiritual and practical aid toward development. For those who wish to learn more, I recommend the book *Creative Color Analysis*, by Mary and some of her students; and/or the website http://www.creativecolor.org, which is overseen by Elizabeth and Fred Kirby.

**MARY**  Every person possesses their own keynote of sound to which they vibrate. Each has a keynote of color which becomes their personal stimulation. Each projects his own aura of color vibrations emanating from within, flowing outward with colors following the contour of the body after the manner of a cocoon, so to speak. The human aura is defined as the Kingdom of the Soul, and the color path is a mystical journey toward development of the soul. In our spiritual life, development comes from within. The soul and spirit of God within each one of us is sometimes called the Tree of Life. Each one of us alone is responsible for its cultivation.

We speak of etheric colors, and we speak of earth colors. Look about you. Step out here on the terrace and count nine shades of green without stopping. The enormous beauty of color, especially here in California, is almost year around. A bird, a single bird will turn its breast up, lift its wing. God put there a touch of color. He made an individual out of a bird even. And so in our Earth world, the Creator didn't stop at small things.

As to etheric colors: it's recognized that out beyond the spectrum of physical sight there exists a large realm of stimuli, which. had we the organism to react to it, many things that today are unknown would become common knowledge. Out beyond these that induce the sense of sight are waves that are more intense and more frequent, but as far as man is concerned, they might as well be nonexistent, for he perceives them not. Through color, we learn to see something that matches our own color. If the sun of our soul is shining forth, we will see our way by the very light of it. Everyone here was shown before we came back into this life what was before us.

Life is eternal. This is the education for the next life. When we once control our heavy emotions we begin living.

**EVA**  I see a lot of color with my spiritual eyes, but I don't see etheric color with my physical eyes. I don't see auras.

**MARY**  Usually it takes a greet deal of development to. But listen, darling, we don't see auras with our physical eyes.

**EVA**  I mean some people see the aura with their eyes open, don't they?

**MARY**  I would say so.

**EVA**  I do see colors; I see lots of color with my eyes closed.

**MARY**  Well, I would be grateful.

**JUNE**  Do colorblind people see color revelations?

**MARY**  Yes, they do. We have colorblind people right in this room now, and they're not color blind at all. They have not found expression. People in the room will tell me they can't sing, but the voice is there; they just haven't acknowledged it or tried to develop it.

**MIRIAM WILLIS**  Development through color eventually means the reading of auras, the hearing of invisible voices, the progression of spiritual talents, and seeing with the spiritual eyes.

**KATHY**  The world calls a person with these abilities a medium. Could we say a medium is a cable from God's world to man's world, a channel? And our Mary is a medium.

**ESTHER BARNES**  To me, Mary is ever so much more than just a medium, no matter that she's extraordinarily clairvoyant. I think of a medium as being the host for a spirit, someone who channels that spirit. Mary, on the other hand, is a seer, one who sees, hears and senses, and is a direct conduit rather than accepting the senses of a spirit.

**MARGARET**  Some people not in these classes have asked me to pigeon hole our teaching. I tell them "esoteric Christianity" that combines elements of all the world's great teachings, and then some!

**ESTHER BARNES**  Definitely "and then some." Because in this class, we receive teachings that are unavailable anywhere else on this Earth!

**PATTI**  Mary, did you receive the Color work and the Planes teaching simultaneously?

**MARY**  No, I didn't. I had my Color work first, and I was told never to give the Planes to anyone that didn't have the Color. But lately, in the last few years, because of the age of Mary Weddell, they relented and said I could use the two together if I felt the person was developed enough to accept it.

**GENE**  Were you always conscious of going over there? As I understand it you have to be very highly advanced before you're conscious of going over.

**LORNA**...Do you know where we're going when you take us out?

**MARY**  I do know where you're going; I've had my direction. As you enter Grand Central Station and there are so many other people there, they all seem to be going somewhere and they seem to know where they're going. We wait silently. Before you know it, we're just lifted and we're where we belong. A great happiness seems to follow us as we approach a temple. For instance, you all know the Temple of Bells, 4$^{th}$ Plane. We'll start humming, our keynotes will come to us, and we blend beautifully. Color and music follow us, and we're helping to create it! Again, when we enter the temple and hear the great organist there, it seems to say everything we need to have said to us. The great and gracious old hymns blend in clouds of music, and as we bask in that, we come clean. By the time we come home, we think we never will break the Law again--which we do. But when we have once entered into this magnificent life, this life of color that flows within and without, it causes us to walk with assurance.

Now, throughout your life you have been praying to someone — someone higher, something whose contact you must make by raising your consciousness. In the Channel, it's no different, other than we're trying to become accustomed to that altitude. In the Channel, we're raising our consciousness to the altitude where Christ walked. He said follow me. It's a growth process; we have to grow with this thought. Faith is the key; we come in faith. Faith is rewarded. Faith enlarges vision; faith enlarges capacity of thinking.

You've heard of this place within since you were children. Sung it in songs, breathed it in prayer. I am the way, the truth, the light. Follow me. All these things you take for granted. We're used to those things. Now we have a ladder that leads up into a vision and in the outreaches of man's consciousness, where he's going to find something he hasn't seen before. As your faith increases your dreams will come through and you will understand them. The reward of faith is to use oneself as proof, your own experience, not someone else's. You're living in a higher level of consciousness and traveling toward the light.

Color can be thought of as a language. Like with any language, you can get by with learning a few words or make it a life-long study in an attempt to master the language. As you go on, the study becomes deeper and more complex.

**MIRIAM WILLIS** ...When beginning to learn the color language, you can pick a few colors and use them to bring harmony to a person, a situation or to oneself. For example, take the color of human love, rosy pink. You can project that color, either through creating it in the mind's eye or directly looking at the color.

**MARY**  Consider the difference of color prayer: it's swifter and more direct than word prayer. Both, however, are good to use.

## The Inner Channel of Our Being
## Twelve Keys to the Kingdom of the Soul

The Inner Channel is a safe, lighted pathway to spiritual development. Your own inner channel is a spiral of etheric substance centered within you at the solar plexus. Each color gives uplift and support to the spiral above it. Because each succeeding color is of a higher vibration than the one below it, you "climb" in consciousness while ascending the Channel. Each time you do so, a little more color is added to your own etheric spiral, and you grow. "Climbing the Channel" is a good way to begin a meditation. As you proceed, draw each color to the inner channel of your being. A focus of one or two seconds on each one, in turn, is sufficient. In whatever way you imagine the Channel—as a ladder, a column of light, spiral stairway, absorbing the colors is what is important.

Beginning with the color of royal purple at the bottom, proceed upward, and either audibly or silently name each color:

"I stand in the royal purple of faith and mount to the gray lavender of the holding force of patience, the pink lavender of inspiration, the rose lavender of the spiritual voice and the blue orchid of prophecy, over the yellow bridge of enlightenment to the rose orchid of the message bearer, the red lilac of the holding force for the Band of Teachers, over the bridge of yellow enlightenment to the glowing peach of union of mind and spirit, the light blue orchid of brotherhood, the blush orchid of serenity, over the bridge of lightest green in desirelessness to the rose bisque of grace and the light blue lavender of peace. And now I stand at the Fount of Supply."

At the word "peace," rest in the quietude of your lifted spirit in silent expectancy. There is great value in this silence. This is a time of communion with the Infinite. You come to the Fount of Supply, to effulgence, and a door opens, a door to the world beyond.

### Keynotes

**MARY WERTI** I don't remember anything we have had concerning an explanation of the different keynotes. I understand your keynote is linked to color, and it's an important part of your life.

**MARY** We come into the world with a keynote. The meaning of that keynote colors the life you live. Your keynote is written in your aura, and the reading is in the color, of course.

**GLENN** Mary, some of the people new to class don't understand that the keynote is the first note that comes out of your throat when you're born.

**MARY** Yes it is; the first cry. It is within the first cry of the babe.

**ANDREW** I notice that some people have the same color, but they'll have a different keynote. So the two don't necessarily relate.

**MARY** They can be different but they do relate. Each combination is a personalized expression of the ego that gives you a personality, an individuality.

**MIRIAM WILLIS** Yes. And the color varies according to the destiny of the person and his development.

**ANDREW** I thought there were certain typical qualities. If anyone had the Keynote of F sharp, for instance, that would indicate that they had certain qualities, just like if Alice Blue was their keynote color, they would have certain qualities.

**MARY**  Yes, they would have certain qualities. Yes indeed, our keynote and keynote color are individualized. We vibrate to our keynote and we are raised in a spiritual vibration. In the Temple of the Bells, in the ringing of those bells you will say, I hear my keynote, and I feel cleansed. And the vibratory likeness of that, when you get on the Other Side and hear the choirs, that's why you come back just absolutely elated because you've never heard such music. They are in their own setting; they're not trying to make the voice or take the note that belongs to anyone else. And so the celestial choirs create music that is way beyond anything we know on earth. We do, once in a while, have string music that could nearly liken unto it, you know.

**MARGARET**  Mary, we either receive our keynote and our keynote color from you, or if we're able, we receive them ourselves in the Temple of Bells on the 4th Plane. Is there another method for receiving one's keynote?

**MARY**  We have the piece by Dr. George, "The Song of Life." Miriam, would you read that part of it, please?

**MIRIAM WILLIS**  "Those who have a good musical ear can determine their keynote by studying the tones of their own voice. Go to the piano and speak in the most natural tone, and then strike note after note until your voice and the note are in perfect accord; then hum and sing this key until every atom of your being is vibrating with it. It will not be long until the vibration of your own voice will open your vision, and color will accompany the tone."

**MARY**  The Temple of Song is a place where sound, color and light are given forth in profusion to uplift, bless, and renew.

**MIRIAM ALBPLANALP**  The Temple of Harmony is also musically important on the Planes.

**JEANNE**  Mary, last night I saw you on the Other Side. You were handing out pitch pipes with keynotes on them and all of them were wrapped in colors. You said something about tacking this onto what we already had, and I received an additional color, which went into all the colors of the Arc of Blue, "Training of the Ego."

**MARY** Very true picture, too. And our pitch pipes went right around the group.

**JEANNE** Is there some reason why tone-deaf people can't carry a tune?

**MARY** It's psychological. It's nothing spiritual. I've been with those people at night on the Other Side, and they sing as lustily as I do.

**JOHN #1** I've run across a lot of people, several whom I've trained to carry a tune. And they've sung in local choirs. It's just a matter of learning to do it.

## Music and Art in Heaven

**PATTI** Is there any particular place on the Other Side where the great music of let us say, Mozart or Bach would be especially heard?

**MARY** Well now, we do have universal temples over there that we go to just for music, where we can go in and sit during the time we're not in classes, and we hear music that is really not only an upliftment, but we bring the evidence of it back with us, because we come back very peaceful.

**LOLA** What about art over there, and the great painters who are on the Other Side?

**MARY** I've told you about the galleries where we go, and there's not only man's accomplishment in the pictures, but the great artists have hung their pictures there because their inspiration came from that particular area. Therefore, you see the original picture, when man's mind tuned in to the spiritual forces and he brought forth something unique and inspirational. We will say that any man who can stay hours working on a canvas and feel elated has worked with spiritual power and not the physical power.

We've known artists who have worked forty-eight hours without food. History has attested to this. And if a man can go that long without being tired, a frail man, a man chiseling on a scaffold, going without food and taking no drink, that means he is lifted out of his physical surroundings for a certain length of time and is endowed with creative energy that does not leave him weak or uncomfortable. And I believe if we can tap that energy, we have so much more to give and so much more to live with.

**JEANNE**   On the Other Side, I've seen art the likes of which I'm sure doesn't exist on Earth, at least not that I've ever seen or heard about. The other night, I saw a unique gold bas relief that glowed in such a way that took my breath away.

**EVA**   Do the great composers play their own works over there?

**MARY**   Oh yes! I remember one Sunday afternoon I was trying to do some work on the other side, and I must have listened to a half hour's concert and when I came back, I was the happiest person you ever knew, and I was able to tell my husband and my mother about it.

**EVA**   Which composers are most active over there? Which ones have you heard, mostly?

**MARY**   Well, I remember the magnificent organs they have there, and Wagner's music, Mendelssohn's music.

**EVA**   Were the composers playing?

**MARY**   Yes. I was going to say the first one I heard was "The Waterfall" by MacDowell, then there was Grieg's music, very light music. It seemed that I mounted the stairs of accomplishment, and before I got through I was listening to the organ and some very heavy music.

**JOHN #1**   Is music changed very much from the original when it's played on the Planes?

**MARY**   We would recognize it. We do form our own personal opinions; they're with us and our memory patterns are with us. So John, you might see a change where I wouldn't. But no one would improve upon a composer in that world!

**ESTHER ESTABROOK**      Are these greet composers creating new compositions there?

**MARY**  That would be from the Pattern World, where you'd go to find that out. Now it might be that they or some of their pupils could be working through to the Earth to bring back some mighty thing, so that we would have some very beautifully created new works coming from this source.

**ESTHER BARNES**  On the Other Side, have the great composers who've gone on composed new masterpieces?

**MARY**  They compose and they are continuing. They compose there the same as they did here, only it's the master's hand, and the art is just beyond. And you have the privilege of going, the same as you do to your museums and concerts here. You have to request it, and you go. And your heart is filled with the beauty of it. And, of course, we come back into a mundane world. And many times we cannot carry it with us, all the things we see.

## CHAPTER THIRTEEN
## MARY ANSWERS CLASS QUESTIONS

**MIRIAM ALBPLANALP**  Our senses are heightened in that world. Can we remember fragrances we smell over there?

**MARY**  You can find out where the fragrance comes from. It's a sign that development is coming to you.

**MIRIAM ALBPLANALP**  Is one of the teachers that comes to us identified by a fragrance close to camphor?

**MARY**  I think there's one, a Greek, who was the creator of camphor. He was medical, and I think he does throw that essence; I've heard that he did. He's quite a talker.

**MIRIAM ALBPLANALP**  I've smelled it several times tonight, and I didn't know how to connect it with our people.

**MARY**  Well, he's a great soul, anyway; he's fine.

**MIRIAM ALBPLANALP**  Mary, this past week I seemed impressed to keep a lighted candle of different colors in the room at night. When you come to pick us up at night is it helpful to you if there's a light in the room?

**MARY**  No. Use the Channel. The lighted candle is a sort of force of adoration.

**MIRIAM ALBPLANALP**  Does that vibration go to the teachers? The guardian angels?

**MARY**  No, you see, they bring their own light with them, dear.

**VIOLET**  Mary, you know how to teach all this because that world is as familiar to you as this world.

**MARY**  Yes, it is.

**HANK**  How many people at a time can be taken over by one teacher?

**MARY**  Well, it's according to the teacher and how many she can handle. In our group, usually we have twenty-one people going over one behind the other. With the people I take over, I would have to come back and forth several times. I come just after twelve o'clock. If I worked in the state of Colorado, if I worked back East, the time would be different. Say that I missed the person, then a teacher would go to the Sleep World and pick that person out of the Sleep World and bring him. Or they might even be there waiting for me, if I miss them. It's a very quick communication, and the movement is very light over there. So I might get there and find the person I might have missed, to my satisfaction, was waiting there for me at the temple gate. So in other words, in God's world everything is order.

**DORIS**  I wondered if there's any sorrowful parting over there, if one is getting ready to come back into the Earth world.

**MARY**  Yes. I've wept many times. I've just wanted to stay so much.

**DORIS**  I don't think I got my question answered, quite. What I meant is, as those who have gone on are getting ready to be reborn into this world, is there a sorrowful parting when they are leaving the Other World to come here?

**MARY**  No, because they've been a long time developing the power to come back and take that responsibility. I'm trying to tell you that there are order and laws which I have had the initiation and know their way of doing it. And I know that I was told by great teachers before I ever took classes that I would get many types of people and that many would think more of their past lives and who they were than they would take the responsibility of living this life. So if I took one and then sent them into the meditative world of the Hindu religion, they could meditate and go back and back and get satisfaction. But they would have left off the living of this life while they were doing that. So that I have never felt that it just, shall I say, putting responsibility off, because this is only a day in school. It's never time enough to get into any kind of good work. There's never time enough to live it. And so to crowd it in is what we need to do. Every day should be one of living.

**GERTRUDE**  If your mother and father were over there, and a brother or sister, and you hear from your mother and dad, why don't you hear from the brother or sister?

**MARY**  Well, how close were you to brother or sister on Earth? Were you as close as you were to your parents?

**GERTRUDE**  No, I never knew them.

**MARY**  It's the tie that binds. They would be developed in an entirely different way, and they would be, probably, even higher than your father and mother, because they've had spiritual training if they went over as children.

**GERTRUDE**  One went over as a baby. Would he be with them now?

**MARY**  No, I don't think so, but if they wanted to, they've been over there long enough they could ask for the privilege of seeing him; you can always see your children.

**JEANNE**  When you go over in the transition of death, there's a big chance you may not have all the same people you had around you on Earth; you might live in an entirely different area, because you were developed in an entirely different way.

**MARY**  Yes, but you can always request to go to where they are, to see them.

**JEANNE**  But you still live apart.

**MARY**  Oh, you live apart. People don't always all live in the same place together, by any means.

**IDA**  Isn't there a chance some of them may be reincarnated?

**MARY**  We're not going to deal with that, Ida, because it takes so many years for those that I've known on the plane of work that I'm doing. I know the story of "accepting incarnation," and I know what it means to go over. But the length of time between, the teachers tell me, is anywhere from a hundred years on up.

**LINDA** I've heard of many people who came back soon. There was one case, listed in a book on reincarnation, a boy stayed over there only five minutes and reincarnated – a very unusual case.

**MARY** I wouldn't know of it, Linda; I'm not that wise. Undeniably, the author of the book you read made a great study of it to be able to receive things like that. I don't believe I am as interested in past lives as some people are. I feel we've enough to worry about with this one life we're living now, and I'm very vitally interested in this life. Because I believe that if we can get the arc of our life, the plan of it and chart our life to that, we're perfectly safe, and we'll have overcome anything we came have to overcome.

**FRANK** I can see that incarnating into a new life might not happen soon after a recent life lived; otherwise, there wouldn't be enough time over there to fully understand all that one learned from the life just lived. But isn't it necessary that we use an entire lifetime to make amends for wrongs of past lives?

**MARY** I don't think we all came to overcome our ill deeds or fashion of life. This is something I've been told over and over again at the Hall of the Akashic Records: that by the time an upright, intelligent, honest person reaches 35 years they have overcome anything from a past life that they've brought along to be overcome.

**MIRIAM WILLIS** Well, you said it rather finally, perhaps, because there are still dispositional things to cultivate.

**MARY** I'm not talking about disposition, I'm talking about those that have committed wrong, have wronged another human being's life, that's based on the thing we've come back to undo. And we can say by the time we're 30 or 35 years old, we will have those past us. We're not carrying any loads at all. I know in the Scrolls that's emphasized at least four times.

**ETHEL** How long does it take a person to know the pattern of his life, or might you call it the plan of his life?

**MARY**  Well, you have to study, you have to seek. You have to lead your life in a certain way to be ready for that. We get it seeing through our development, developing the Channel and seeking our way clearly, by self control, the purification of the mind and body. It comes just naturally to us. It's not something you can buy the plan of, or anything like that. I mean to say, you cannot know— because there has to be a seed planted, and it has to grow. It's slow, but I can see the third eye developing in people. And that means that you will start hearing and seeing things that you should.

**GENE**  When a person gets to a certain plane, does that mean that he no longer has to reincarnate on Earth?

**MARY**  That's something that's different for each individual. You might have not fulfilled the law that you came to fulfill, or you might desire to come back again and fulfill something. You might desire to come back to Earth to teach something that was very vital to others.

**PATTI**  Mary, you've been privileged to know many planes beyond the ones we go to in our night work, but are those higher planes inhabited as well?

**MARY**  To me, Patti, it's very evident that people live and have their being on all these planes, the ones we go to as well as the higher planes beyond where we go.

**PATTI**  Several of the great religions and philosophies of the world speak of three or five or seven heavens which go up to Supreme God Consciousness. I was wondering is there anything in our Planes work that can fit that in? For example, are there a thousand Planes of Heaven—or how many are there?

**MARY**  Up to the Heaven World that I know, there's at least a hundred planes that I've seen and known, and I've known teachers from the 300th Plane. But I know there are far more planes than that.

**MIRIAM WILLIS**  Jesus is said to be from the 2000th Plane.

**PATTI**  To the first Heaven, and then, after that ...

**MARY**  I don't see them that way. I haven't been privileged to see them that way. Mine is Heaven and Earth, and they are one, in one great circle. That's the way I was shown it, and then from there, there are planes, as if we were climbing.

**JEANNE**  I wanted to ask about that. Is it a set space, or is it expanding all the time?

**MARY**  It's expanding. Expanding where my eyes would not reach, where my imagination could not go, but I expect to see farther out, more circumference, when I have developed to the place where I can do so. I believe that man develops all there is to see, but he has to evolve to do it.

**MARGARET**  These planes, these temples are just like the "many mansions" of the New Testament, as Jesus said: "For in my father's house are many mansions."

**MIRIAM WILLIS**  How many planes are there? An infinite number, to be sure. The highest plane of reality is unfathomable, but as seekers, we continually progress towards the goal of knowing.

**VONNIE**  Where do people go when under sedation?

**MARY**  They go to what we would call a netherland. There's a great sleep land that is in the next registered realm or area, we'll say. And it's closer to the center, above the Magnetic Field on the 1st Plateau. They are "detained" as it were, "held", and there's no particular suffering, but sometimes they will have bad dreams from whatever the dosage is they take.

**IDA**  Can you tell me the difference between a soul and a spirit?

**MARY**  "Soul" is the body of God, in sight, or in us. "Spirit" is the essence of, or the Holy Ghost, as they call it, the essence of, or the aroma of God's love. That's the way it was given to me.

**IDA**  The astral body is the soul?

**MARY**  The astral body fits around the soul. The soul is the light.

**IDA**  The Spirit is the "perfect us."

**MARY**  We're expressing the soul that he placed within us! And it lives within the spiritual body, which is within us. We lay the old body down and go over and have the spiritual body to live in.

**HELEN VON GEHR**  Is that spiritual body a counterpart of the physical body?

**MARY**  It is very much more beautiful.

**MIRIAM WILLIS**  This might be a good time for me to read Mary's teaching on "The Spiritual Body, the Three Bodies, the Soul." If I may, Mary:

"Spiritual Body - The garment of the soul, used while living here on Earth as body vehicle for the soul when it leaves the physical body in sleep. It is a consciousness put on by the soul as it leaves the physical body. It dwells in the Heaven World when not in use in invisible form. For one who has become a master of the law and forces of the universe, this spiritual body of his can be brought to him through the raising of vibrations and the desire of the soul, and thus clothing the soul or entity, it makes possible the going anywhere of that person in service as a disciple of the Christ and Master of development. This spiritual body is universal. Each soul has its own, but its beauty and development is achieved by the living of a life of selflessness, in accord with the fundamental laws of love, given us by the Christ's life and teaching. Events, emotions, thought and all else, can be raised to the level of the consciousness of this spirit or highest self.

"The Three Bodies and Emotions or Desire. - There can develop a perfect balance between the three bodies which man possesses (physical, mental, spiritual). The mental, or thought one, maintains equilibrium or balance in the emotional realm, between the physical and the spiritual, so that one can remain on the ray of power. Raising emotion, including love, to this third or highest body, brings a peace, adjustment to life's trials and tests, and also brings spiritual growth. Training through a teacher, knowledge gained in night work, caring and help given by one's guides, and the 'channel of divine power' are the priceless gifts to balance control of the emotional bodies.

"The Soul - There is in each person a white light which is 'the light of the soul.' The Soul leaves the body through the top of the head. To be conscious of our soul is to feel joy. The spirit is the active element of the Soul. The Soul gathers around itself elements which make it individual. It's the power of love which gives us this teaching. One far enough advanced can see this light, the holy breath of Spirit."

**MIRIAM ALBPLANALP**   Mary, I've always felt these planes were all more or less different states of consciousness, and if I reach a certain state of consciousness in this part of our country and someone in the middle of China receives the same state of consciousness, wouldn't we be on the same spiritual plane?

**MARY**   You'd be in the same spiritual plane through the Planes of Heaven.

**HELEN MARSH**   But don't we have to get there?

**MARY**   If we're going out in the spiritual body, it's a different thing. Then the Afterlife is a state of consciousness. When we're over in our night work it is Reality, and this, Earth, is the shadow. It's just reversed, because we're in our spiritual body.

**SYLVIA**   If a person had a great talent and for some reason weren't able to develop or use that talent, yet the longing remained, would they have the privilege of fulfilling that on the Other Side, or do they have to wait until they reincarnate?

**MARY**   I believe with the development that is in this room, no one needs to come back for another life unless they want to, which means you work out your future development from the plan of Heaven, and that all the things you've left undone here or that you have the desire to do will be fulfilled over there.

**GLENN**   I know several people in the group are wondering how high on the planes can you go on this Earth. To what level?

**MARY**   Well, I wouldn't be the one to judge, but let me say I've known teachers here on earth for whom we've had memorial services, who were welcomed to a certain plane over there. There are a number of them, I think at least five, who have gone to the 120th Plane. They were working here on Earth, and you surely wouldn't have recognized where they were on the planes, because they lived simple lives.

**JEANNE**   When these spiritual teachers came into this particular life, would they come in as a 1st Plane soul, or would they already be up?

**MARY**   They start as a child and rise from there into their fullest possibility.

**GLENN**   That's just the question. Do they start back on the 1st Plane, or do they come in with a higher plane?

**MARY**   No matter what plane you come in on, the knowledge that you have, you're still the child in need of learning when you come in. Buried in that soul is the knowledge you need if you want to search for it, but it's like having oil on your property, Glenn, if you don't dig for it, you don't have anything.

**SYLVIA**   Is there any chance a 20th Plane person would come back and not make it back up to the 20th Plane?

**MARY**   Oh my, yes! But any person who has made the 20th Plane and comes back here never loses the right to that 20th Plane on the other side of life, because they've grown to that degree, and any one thing we receive as a degree of improvement in this life is added. It's called the treasure and Christ spoke of it many times, in laying our treasure in Heaven. So it's the deeds we do and then facing ourselves and knowing what we are inside. No matter what the front is that we give to other people, we will almost know by the very recognition where we were when we came, and whether we're improving or not.

If a person is a 20th Plane person when they come in, they can go back over there and they will be no further than the 2nd Plane as far as what they have done on Earth. This is a day in school. This Earth counts! Because we have to redeem ourselves in the sight of God, we go under redemption every night of our lives that we come up before God's table of questions, for the teachers ask these questions, which is a revelation in itself.

**GLENN**  To get it real plain, then, a 20th Plane person comes back to this life. If they bumble along and progress as far as the 8th Plane here, then when they go back to the next world, they're still on the 20th Plane?

**MARY**  No, they would be on the 28th Plane. They have made eight planes more. It's very like our credits in the university. All the way through our schools, and on through college.

**DORIS**  Mary, I want to ask about seeing faces in meditation or before going to sleep at night, or upon waking. If one sees faces, could they be from the lower planes?

**MARY**  No! Excuse me. When we get to the end of the Channel, there is supposed to be a door that we push open into the next that world, and faces will welcome us. Sometimes they're teachers that you've never seen; sometimes they're teachers of another life, and they greet you by name. Other times, there's mothers, fathers, sisters, brothers, a familiar one, which is the loveliest thing that can happen to you.

**DORIS**  It couldn't be someone from the lower planes?

**MARY**  I don't believe that anyone who has ever been in my classes and gone into the Channel has seen an ugly face. If so, I would like to know it. If you have had an experience in life of having a very ugly time with someone, that is buried in what they call "subconscious," and at such a time when you get into a refined atmosphere you will feel to the depths of your being that you want to throw off that load. There may be a guilt that carries that face in your consciousness. Many people have bitterly disliked someone, and then they naturally forget it because they don't care to remember. But there are times when that reflection just right out of the blue comes to you. That's the time that I would certainly use the height of Color.

**MIRIAM WILLIS**  It stands as a barrier between you self and God himself if you have hated someone. And your selfishness here has to be corrected there.

**MARY**  When a face comes before you, my students, send that person love. And on the wings of love, they will awaken to something new within them, and you will be blessed, because that which goes out and dwells in the heart of another comes back to you. Everything is in circles. And the cycle of understanding will come to you in the same way, and you will be awakened to the needs of your own life, and your soul will feel those needs. We were meant to face this; it was our problem and no one else's. Therefore, as we turn and go back, which we always do, we will meet that same person back there somewhere or a condition similar. For if a person dodges a responsibility once in their life, I assure you it will came back again. That same thing will return, dressed in a different garb–for you to face it.

Always look for the thing in yourself that bothers you in the other person. It's a simple formula, but oh, it works wonderfully. Well, that's one little burden I've lain down, because you're learning from these people day by day. And every time that little thing comes up that irks you, you have spent some energy. And that energy is being pulled from the spiritual body, because you haven't excess energy in your mental body. You're fighting in your mental body, so if there's any energy that is taken, it's pulled from that lying dormant there, and every time we pull this energy out we have wasted this little network of spiritual love that is being set up as a protective net around us. And that's where our Color rests, and that's when I say, throw on your robe of purple and have faith. It's because a network of the spiritual life is thrown around us.

We look back on our life and we can see the most enjoyable spots in that life, if we want to look for that. Then we go into the Halls of Remembrance, and it brings joy and it brings sorrow. And you do wonder, why in the world did I make that mistake? What led up to it? In some cases it's a lack of sensitivity.

As we walk this Path of Enlightenment, you'll be surprised how all of these things return. We accept the power that can be given to us can easily adjust to the ebb and flow of another person's thinking. As you test yourselves for that, the greatest frustration in your life comes from disagreement—with what you read, what you hear, what someone else does who thinks differently than you. And you again examine yourself and say, why am I thinking that I should color the mind of another human being? People can live together in harmony if one doesn't dominate the other with their thoughts. If we expect to become developed people, then more and more we arrive at the place where we have few ruts to display before others.

**PATTI** In order to help a loved one who leaves us to go on to the Other Side, is there a best way to dispose of the physical remains?

**MARY** As far as interment is concerned, the expense of it nowadays is a hardship on many people. So let's say it makes no difference. That spiritual body is still there, waiting for you. That is the eternal thing, the body eternal we live in. So whichever way we do it, let us know it's fine. In past ages, in other cultures, they were burned – there were great pyres – the higher the pyre the greater the honor in those olden days, the greater the person; and ashes to ashes is said through the service. To wait a few days is almost a holy rite. Whether it's just a fallacy, I can't say. I've always felt they should have that much respect to wait, not to be in a hurry. There are many lines of thought. Christ was entombed, and as a Christian, perhaps that's where I got that. But with the crowded nations we have, with the many people dying that have to be interred, where is the ground? This body is not sacred, the soul is sacred and the soul is given a new body. No matter who they are, when they go over, there is still a spiritual body for them; remember that.

**RALPH** Does waiting three days, as some religions recommend, have anything to do with the silver cord?

**MARY** No. When life ends, that cord is broken.

**BILL ESTABROOK** How do you feel about displaying the body after death?

**MARY** I don't believe my ideas on the subject would be worthwhile, because there's an association of morticians that do as they please. You and I would say in due respect to that body, if we're going to show it, let's be honest about this; if the person has died of a heart attack, it turns very quickly. If a mortician comes in and takes care of that body immediately after death, then that body can be seen and it isn't a hideous swollen mass where blood has come to the surface.

**LINDA** On the Other Side, if one is sent on a certain mission, would they clothe themselves in the colors which were advantageous to the power needed?

**MIRIAM ALBPLANALP** I often wondered about such things. Am I going to look like I look now in the dress I'm wearing today when we go out tonight?

**MARY** It's according. We nearly all, as a color group, wear robes of soft materials, Grecian robes; they just wrap around us and we're on our way. We clothe ourselves from our mental pictures.

**ALMA** Isn't it true that we just don't leave a plane and never come back to it?

**MARY** No, we always return.

**KATHY** Could you make it clearer for me? Is not being able to distinguish between sight and what is being given to you and your own imagination a matter of disbelief?

**MARY** I would have to just simply say to take it on faith. I think intelligence must always be used in any message we receive. We must know that our mind was clear, and that our desire body was out of it.

**KATHY** Well, perhaps you weren't looking for anything, something just came, and you assumed you were having a beautiful, delightful daydream? But tonight I realized that I have already seen the Temple of Receptivity, and never realized it.

**MARY** That's due to being taken out. You're touching Reality for once! And just be grateful that you have it!

**MIRIAM WILLIS** Mary, it's "growing in recognition of it."

**MARY** Yes, that's what I'm trying to say. You have received, and you recognized what you received.

**DORIS** I have absolutely no imagination. It's either there or isn't, and for me it isn't. But suddenly I just saw all this beautiful purple. It was just pure purple, almost an indigo.

**MARY** You have been initiated into Faith.

**DORIS** And then suddenly, that pure purple morphed into this astounding rose purple almost amethyst color of divine imagination. It was something so unexpected; it was just scintillating there before my eyes.

**GENE** I would like to know, when one of your students asks you something and you say, "I don't know, but I'll find out," what is the process that you go through to get the information? Could you answer that?

**MARY** Well, I might be a little more fortunate, as I'm quite used to the way back and forth between where I go for my information than my student is, or they'd have it themselves. It's not that I'm preferred. It's simply that I have followed the Path a long time. And I wouldn't answer the question if I didn't feel the student needed it. And then I would leave it up to the Hierarchy, where I would ask my question to be answered. I would always check the aura around the person before I take something on as a serious question. And then at night when we go over, I would go to the Hierarchy, and I'd put my question there. It would have to be something that was real, something that would benefit the person who asked or the person he was asking it for.

**PATTI** I have a question. I have an enormous amount of energy just as I'm ready to go to sleep. I feel too keyed up spiritually to sleep.

**MARY** I couldn't advise you to use any more energy in the daytime than you do. What time did you go into meditation?

**PATTI** Probably too late.

**MARY** Then try doing your meditation earlier for awhile, and see how that works.

**PATTI** I thought perhaps there was some virtue in this; one is alone, it's very quiet late at night.

**MARY** Very tempting, but I don't know that you should lose four hours' sleep at this time. We'll try earlier.

**ESTHER ESTABROOK** What happens to a person who has a restless night and sleeps about a half hour and wakens and goes back to sleep?

**MARY** Well, you see, it isn't as it is here. Your time—if you're really in a class and you're working, you're picked up by a teacher and taken to that class. And if you only stay a half hour, you get a half hour of that class. But you usually put in your two hours over there. And you always have enough work that you bring back a picture or dream that can create for you your own picture. That's what the development is. The development should he such that the inner you is opened, and on the camera of your life will be placed that lens you will be looking through in the early morning, and you will see something. And then, write it down and go on. It will come just instantly that way.

**MARGARET** Our favorite Japanese friend is either on the Other Side or expected shortly. Will she be able to go from the Japanese people to the United States people whom she dearly loves as easily as she has here?

**MARY** Yes, Peggy, there's no color over there.

**MARGARET** But can she cross this fortified national line any time she likes?

**MARY** If she asks to do it.

**MARGARET** Where would be her natural home?

**MARY** According to where she lived on this Earth. If her habitat has been with Americans, then she probably will naturally form that association. There's nothing to debar her but herself.

**JOHN #1** On the 13th Plane and above, you say there is neither Gentile nor Jew; you say the Hindus join with us. Do they accept Christ?

**MARY** No, they accept their own teacher. Our Christ was a teacher to us, and Buddha was their teacher and their example; he lived an exemplary life. I could take you through many teachers, so there's a place where all men meet up with God.

**LOLA** If we merge with others on the 13th Plane, do others also go to the same Hierarchy we do? Do we go to a different hierarchy at some point?

**MARY** No, we never change.

**DOROTHY** When we're told we have new teachers, is that an advancement?

**MARY** It's an advancement.

**GENE** Pardon me for being curious, but I'd like to know about your other groups. I've heard we're not the only people you take out at night, nor are we the only group you meet with during the week.

**ESTHER BARNES** Yes, Mary, we've heard you have a group from Europe that comes over every other year and spends an entire year with you. Is that true?

**MARY** Yes, it is.

**MARGARET** We heard these groups are people from England and France.

**MIRIAM WILLIS** Yes, indeed, these people come to Mary from across the ocean, and they do stay one full year. Some of them are teaching Mary's color course in London and Paris. When they're back there, they communicate with us by letter and sometimes by telephone.

**GENE** And of course at night on the Planes.

**MARY** I've been very close to another group, an older group than you people. There were 80 of them when we started, 59 now, and those couples ... one passes, then another passes; there's solace in calling Mary. They know, in other words, it's just like calling Mother. I thank God I have that capacity to hear and see them. Vicariously, I'm in that same spot with them, whatever their trouble is.

**LENORE** The mentally ill, do they get well faster over there?

**MARY** No, they do not. It's a very slow process, and it takes a great many teachers to get the mentally ill over it, because they're no longer mentally ill, but you have to make them believe that. And of course, that's true in many of the things that are wrong with us here. We believe it, and therefore, it is so.

**MIRIAM WILLIS** If we could only unbelieve it.

## MAP/CHART II - THE 1ST AND 2ND PLANES OF HEAVEN

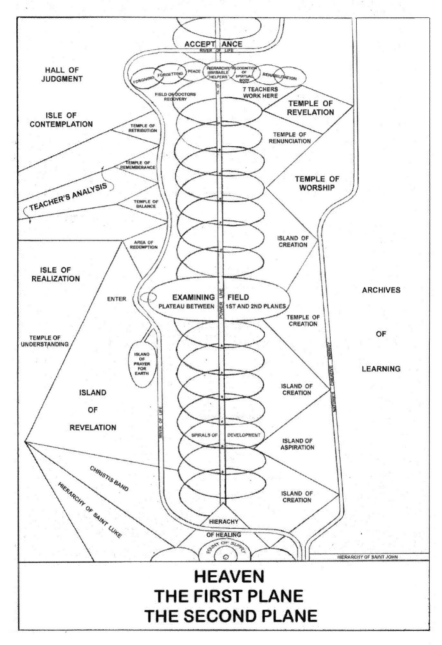

# POINTS OF INTEREST
# ON THE 1ST AND 2ND PLANES OF HEAVEN

**1st Plane**

1. Fount of Supply
2. Hierarchy of St. John
3. Hierarchy of St. Luke
4. Hierarchy of Healing
5. Christis Band
6. Island of Creation
7. Island of Aspiration
8. Island of Revelation
9. Isle of Realization
10. Temple of Understanding
11. Temple of Creation
12. Island of Prayer for Earth
13. Archives of Learning

**Plateau Between 1st and 2nd Planes**

14. Examining Field

**2nd Plane**

15. Island of Creation
16. Archives of Learning
17. Teachers' Analysis
18. Area of Redemption
19. Temple of Worship
20. Temple of Balance
21. Temple of Remembrance
22. Temple of Renunciation
23. Temple of Revelation
24. Temple of Retribution
25. Temple of Renunciation
26. Isle of Contemplation
27. Hall of Judgment

28. Field of Doctors' Recovery
29. 7 Teachers
30. Forgiving
31. Forgetting
32. Peace
33. Recognition of Spiritual Body
34. Rehabilitation
35. Hierarchy of Invisible Helpers
46. Acceptance

# CHAPTER FOURTEEN
# PRELUDE TO THE FIRST TWO PLANES OF HEAVEN

**MARY** You're such fine students, but these first planes are unfamiliar to you. You're more aware of the planes beyond these. I think it's a resistance you've had in the past of taking on the first planes. You've read Indian philosophy, Theosophy and so forth, and many teachings take you to meditation on the 8$^{th}$ Plane.

**MIRIAM WILLIS** Perhaps by the grace of God and the number of opportunities we've had, we may be farther along the path than this chart of the 1$^{st}$ and 2$^{nd}$ Planes. Nevertheless, there are many who must travel through these paths of learning, so it's well for us to understand more about them. On the maps of Heaven, on the charts, you can see where the temples belong, how we make our ascent through these temples for the development of the soul, and how this information does enlighten us.

**MARY** The first four Planes of Heaven are of a preparatory and probationary nature, a clearing up of misconceptions and avoiding jumping to conclusions. The right side of a plane is the active side. In playing a more active role, we review our actions. The left side is that of the seeker, the receptive side where we receive more teaching and instruction. We go back and forth many times from left to right on these maps, or vice versa, getting power on one side to go back and learn or do tests on the other.

**FRANK** What's the difference between a plateau and a plane?

**MARY** Plateaus are areas located between planes. Their purpose is to review what we have learned on the previous plane and to prepare for the next plane. We're tested on the qualities we have developed on the plane just completed and are helped to integrate knowledge gained. Each test must have built into the stature of the soul the degree of refinement needed for that level of development.

**MIRIAM WILLIS** Our soul consciousness is ahead of our Earth consciousness. After having tests on the Other Side, we will have Earth tests equal to our soul attainment in order to bring the bodies into balance. When they're in balance we can go on to the next plane.

**BILL JACKSON**   May I ask, what are the lines shown on the chart? I mean also the spirals and the other lines. What do they represent?

**MARY**   The lines and spirals on the charts represent invisible meridians of power energy – life force. There are 7 spirals central in each map of the first six planes. These must be climbed and 7 tests tried and passed on each spiral before we can go higher. The tests on these stations function to meet the need of each individual and their purpose is to advance his growth. These spirals build power in preparation for graduating to the 3$^{rd}$ Plane, where if one has earned it, he will find his home.

**MIRIAM WILLIS**   This home is built of the good deeds in the Earth life just left. It may be a cottage or a castle according to the life one has lived on Earth. This is his treasure in Heaven. The Master said, "Lay up for yourselves treasures in Heaven."

**ESTHER BARNES**   A temple is a higher vibration than an island, I believe. And islands are higher in vibration than isles.

**MIRIAM WILLIS**   There may be a fine distinction between the two names, but in the main they reflect the need for instruction in changing attitudes, behavior and preconceived ideas of the higher realms.

**MARY**   We might well say these isles and islands are a prerequisite to visiting and partaking of the splendor that lies ahead in the Heaven World.

**ANDREW**   These islands that occur, four on the 1$^{st}$ Plane – what is the function of those islands?

**MARY**   The function of the islands is to clear souls of their habits of prejudices and biased thinking. The Islands of Creation are areas to which we go many times, and always the experience provides new wonders and inspires greater aspiration.

**MIRIAM WILLIS**   On the 1$^{st}$ Plane there is the Island of Creation, which occurs again on the 2nd Plane. It is indeed an indoctrination into a new world where new standards of measure confront us as we go.

**MARY** The islands are places of quiet. We go apart to be made over, a first step toward that higher goal of being reborn.

**LINDA** Do we learn a great deal about the origin of life there?

**MIRIAM WILLIS** We continually seek for proof and evidence of the other world. This can be substantiated in the Islands of Creation located on the 1st and 2nd Planes, right side.

**LINDA** And the isles? What is their chief feature?

**MIRIAM WILLIS** These isles have an atmosphere of nature's vibrant beauty about them. They herald the persuasion to look up; "be ye lifted up."

**MARY** There are many splendid buildings in these areas with beautiful gardens, green lawns, a wide variety of trees, much symmetry and balance. One can easily find secluded places in which to ponder. One is always attracted to the place which one needs on each particular occasion.

**ESTHER ESTABROOK** What about the Halls of Learning?

**MIRIAM WILLIS** You could say they're similar to our colleges and universities, as a huge variety of knowledge is taught there. Those who have set opinions find an expansion toward a more universal aspect of life. This is often a slow process, for habits of thinking cling and tend to return even when loosened.

**MARY** But as desire for expansion of thinking grows so the power to do so is given according to the ability to receive. In this way expansion of thinking is experienced, the error faced and overcome, and weakness strengthened until the habit or old mold is broken. To live in immortality now is the greater challenge, for this reiterates the concept of One Great World and One Intent.

# CHAPTER FIFTEEN
# THE 1ˢᵀ PLANE OF HEAVEN

On the 1st Plane we find two Islands of Creation, the Island of Revelation, the Island of Realization, Island of Aspiration, Island of Prayer for Earth, the Christis Band, and the Temple of Understanding, Temple of Creation, the Examining Field, Halls of Learning, and the Archives of Learning. The 1st Plane offers the opportunity for greater adjustment to the life and its conditions for discarnate souls. While there are several islands on this plane, there are few temples, namely the Temple of Understanding at the left of the Spirals of Development, and the Temple of Creation, which is at the upper right hand side of the Spirals. The Islands of Creation are areas to which one goes many times, where the experience always provides new wonders and inspires greater aspirations.

**ESTHER ESTABROOK** It isn't clear to me what the purpose of the 1st Plane is.

**MARY** The 1st Plane is one of adjustment and examining. We go out of this life, and let's say we're not informed. When you are ready, you go into the Examining Field on the 1st Plane. And there you're asked the questions, and you go back again and again as one set of teachers after another ask you questions; they examine your life as you have lived it, asking about this and that incident. And if you have not had this kind of training, you're wondering where did they get this information? You almost feel as if they'd been spying on you.

Souls who progress to the 1st Plane discover a two-fold truth: the personal aspect of self unfoldment experienced in the tests on the Spirals of Development, and an opportunity to grow in the realization of the wonders of Creation, which begin to unfold on the Island of Creation. 1st Plane teaching is brief and takes the form of a defense of one's character. Many who reside in Restland come here for the purpose of learning through growth and adjustment to happier, more comfortable living in this different state. For some this is difficult, requiring frequent visits and testings. As many visits as needed are granted them.

Appropriately enough, the 1st Plane contains a reminder of the creation of all life. True evidence is found here, as the soul is shown the many processes of life from the unformed, invisible, life-giving energy to the birth or development of sound, form, and color vibrant with life and beauty. The seeker is especially impressed by the intricacy and reality of this process, resulting in the harmonious order of creation, adding dimension in evolutionary growth. One sees the act of causing to exist or of being brought into existence by divine power, especially the act of bring the universe into existence. This concept is repeated over and over from one plane to another with deepening expansion of consciousness. There is a provision for souls to grow in appreciation of their own being. They are privileged to go to this Island again and again to deepen self-respect and to learn much concerning the marvels of creation.

From these experiences they earn the right to go to the Island of Revelation, where one receives the power to investigate and pursue the quest still further. Progress made thus far is revealed to him, and he is shown more clearly the path ahead, including his personal needs toward further growth in knowledge and ordered attainment in his life and environment, for he has to live in the rhythm of the order of over there to be able to sustain the dimension of the light. The Island of Revelation discloses to us our shortcomings and the extent to which we have fallen short of measuring up to our responsibilities in relation to our fellow men.

**MIRIAM WILLIS** There's an act of revealing and discovery of divine truth, especially the truth of self hitherto unknown, a disclosure of man's self to himself in the light of divine truth. The Isle of Revelation (left side of the chart/map) is particularly important for disclosing and discovering such truths.

**MARY** The self is revealed to the extent of its capacity to understand. Desire brings one to the Isle of Aspiration (above and to the right on the map). Here, one breathes in the power to become more inspired, receiving through his desire to investigate and pursue his quest further.

**MIRIAM WILLIS** An awakened consciousness wishes to know more, and through desire, their powers are stimulated to learn yet more.

**MARY**  When the soul receives encouragement in seeing the progress he's made and is shown more clearly the path ahead, he realizes he must live in a higher dimension and grow in knowledge. He sees truths about himself hitherto unknown, which may be excellent qualities he didn't know he had, or may be pretty heavy blows, things that he didn't realize. This is truly a disclosure of himself in the light of divine truth.

**ANDREW**  Do isles, islands and temples perform similar functions but in differing degrees?

**MARY**  That's right. It's interesting to observe the progression of unfoldment as one climbs higher in development. At the Island of Aspiration, we come face to face with what we've become.

**MIRIAM WILLIS**  On the Isle of Realization, we're confronted with the words: "a charge I have to keep," and we ask ourselves to what extent has this been kept? We're also reminded to keep human emotions in check. If you become critical, you suddenly find yourself alone in a lower dimension until you're ready to acknowledge your flaw and seek correction.

**MARY**  There's no camouflage at all. There's nothing you can get by with. It's the essence of truth and reality. Whereas here on Earth we can cover up, deceive and get by, and many people feel it's all right if you don't get caught, that kind of false standard is unacceptable over there.

**LOLA**  Mary, would you say something about the Island of Prayer for Earth?

**MARY**  The Island of Prayer for Earth (left side of the map) is an island of prayer power. Fervent prayers received from the Earth are purified and reinforced with additional power. Earth prayers ascended are multiplied in power, evoking the help of Heaven in fulfilling God's will. No prayers are lost after they go through here.

**VIOLET**  We haven't mentioned the Temple of Understanding yet.

**MIRIAM WILLIS**  On the 1$^{st}$ Plane, we have the first Temple of Understanding. The purpose of all Temples of Understanding, which are located on many planes, is to clarify to the mind, bring to fuller understanding the working centers of consciousness in both the physical and the spiritual body.

**MARY** This temple reveals the meaning of one's life to the height of the seeker's capacity. It's where the roots, the basic reasons for a state or condition are made clear, enabling the discarnate to understand the condition of life they now live in, and adjust to it.

**MIRIAM WILLIS** This adjustment is difficult for those who haven't thought there is existence after death, or perhaps had no belief in a great Creator, or at least had not really thought about this while on Earth.

**MARGARET** Isn't it true that we the living can take our problems of the day to this temple at night while we're on this side of life?

**MARY** That's right. The Temple of Understanding is for both discarnate souls and for souls who journey forth from their Earth body at night for spiritual development. You're shown your power to grow through spiritual adventure in balanced faith. Asking God to give you an understanding heart, you find a new supply of devotion and a broader perspective of life in this temple. For both ourselves and the discarnate, the necessities for progress in this divine adventure are forgiveness, silence, serenity, and justice. Living in harmony opens new doors to development. Here we face these questions: Do we understand who we are and where we're going? Have we in the past been indifferent? Has apathy stood in our way?

**MIRIAM WILLIS** The power is furnished to quicken and deepen one's relationship to others in sympathy and without criticism.

**MARY** Every soul goes here to begin the climb to the Mount of Renunciation. As the soul further develops, one will look back at the 1$^{st}$ Plane and distinctly see thirteen distinguishing colors, as well as many intermediate shades which bridge the evolutionary spaces between the different strata.

**MIRIAM WILLIS** We're responsible not only in our choices but for providing the building materials which will be used in our heavenly dwelling places. So in the Temple of Understanding, the power to understand more deeply is presented.

**MARY** It's the power of perception of ideas, the power to distinguish, dealing with impressions, composing them into wholeness of comprehension.

**HELEN MARSH** I had a recall, part of which I believe comes from the Temple of Understanding. I was standing on a high rise of ground. Down below me was a large pond of beautiful blue water, and over on my right was an oblong building in a sort or golden marble tone with a frieze around it. To my left was a semi circular building with six columns around the outer edge, set in a green meadow. As I woke up I had just come out of a rectangular temple to my left. Someone was walking by a six foot high wall with an opening between it and the temple. There was a beautiful lawn decked with trees with the sun shining on it.

**MARY** The Temple of Understanding is a great rectangular building, and it provides a true understanding of man and his needs. It's what I call "the basic temple." It has the great door most temples have.

**EVELYN** You mentioned indifference. Isn't that one of the hardest things to overcome?

**MARY** Yes, and we certainly can't afford to be indifferent. Indifference is considered one of the greatest sins, and as you say, being indifferent is very hard to overcome. You have to have the heart open in the sight of God before you ever get creative energy pouring through and really living within it.

**MIRIAM WILLIS** There's another area just below the 1st Plane in the triangle over at the right side of the chart, the Training Field for Night Work.

**MARY** We go there before we can go anywhere else, to have the chemistry of the spiritual body develop so that we're strong enough to go farther. That's not so very far along the way, is it? And many times we would go back there and seek.

**MIRIAM WILLIS** All of these temples appear on many planes. They repeat, and we learn and absorb many things concerning these conditions, up to the level of our unfoldment or development.

**MARY**  All such temples reveal ourselves to ourselves.

# CHAPTER SIXTEEN
# THE 2ND PLANE OF HEAVEN

The many temples of the 2nd Plane, beginning on the left side of the map/chart, include: The Temple of Redemption, dedicated to redeeming mankind; the Temple of Balance, where we learn to live with balanced emotions; the Temple of Remembrance, which reminds us of the things we have forgotten to do and forgotten what we were endowed with; the Temple of Retribution, which indicates the necessity of retribution – otherwise, no peace.

Temples on the right side of the map/chart include: The Temple of Worship, where our weekly life record is placed upon the altar and reverberates back to us on our own wave length; the Temple of Renunciation, where we lay aside nonessential things – which are in reality retardants to our spiritual growth; Temple of Revelation, where self is revealed to self, for of truth, "all things are known."

Notice there are five principles in five temples that begin with "Re" (Revelation, Remembrance, Retribution, Renunciation, and Redemption). In Greek, re means going into, as to contemplate. Action on the 2nd Plane is very illustrative of the book, *Pilgrim's Progress*, and fulfills the same mission.

**MARY**  As you read these maps of Heaven, these charts, you'll see where the temples belong, how we make our ascent through them for the development of the soul, and how this information does enlighten us.

**WOODIE**  The 1st Plane looks like it's building the person up to face the 2nd Plane, and the 2nd Plane seems to be doing the same thing all over again.

**JOHN #1**  Does the 2nd Plane have a particular designation? Is it known as a plane of something or other?

**MARY**  If it has a general theme, it might be contemplation.

**MIRIAM WILLIS**  The 2nd Plane is designed to provide for the neglects and failures of life. On this plane is the Isle of Contemplation, where we re-evaluate teachings and truths are imparted. In a great stillness, we deeply consider the many things that are revealed in these temples. Here also our powers of contemplation are fed and deepened.

**MARY**   The Isle of Contemplation is provided for souls to deeply consider all things that would hinder progress. Our blind spots are revealed. Our work here goes beyond the mental level to still the mind in meditation as we clear our souls of habits of prejudice and biased thinking.

**MIRIAM WILLIS**   The 2nd Plane contains another Island of Creation. Here original ideas are born and brought into creation on Earth, something that is of benefit to humanity in healing, usefulness, or beauty. Such things are then recorded in the Pattern World on the Subplane.

**MIRIAM ALBPLANALP**   There's the Temple of Creation here, too.

**MIRIAM WILLIS**   The very first thing we learn there is reverence for all created things, to realize the source of all life, and one great supply of energy expressed in vastly different forms of consciousness.

**GLENN**   Isn't it on this plane that we're shown how the entire world was created?

**MARY**   That's right.

**ESTHER BARNES**   Continuing with locations on the 2nd Plane, may we speak about the Temple of Redemption?

**MIRIAM WILLIS**   The soul awakens to his need and is given cleansing power enabling him to go to Temple of Redemption, where he is presented with the opportunity to redeem himself by reinventing his motives to receive the enabling, healing power of redemptive force. In this Temple he begins to experience the change in his life from waste to gain through the transforming power of redeeming grace. We become more aware of the source of power to give and receive. We have talents we haven't recognized. We face the reality of who we truly are.

**MARY**  This brings man to the Temple of Balance where he sees the causes of his imbalance and is given power to grow to truer balance. He is taught how to recreate his forces, to become more poised and controlled in his emotions so that he learns to live in balance in body, mind and soul.

**MIRIAM WILLIS**  Fear is a source of imbalance. But here we're trained in being centered to keep on the power ray in leaving the body at night and living in balance by day, freed from moods of depression, criticism, bias and prejudice. Here one grows in the desire to live in radiance.

**BERNARD**  Regarding the Temple of Balance: This relates to the Buddha, whose teaching involves the contemplation of the nirvanic state of desirelessness. There is the story of an individual who came to the Buddha and asked, would you teach me what is the source of salvation? The Buddha said follow me. He took the man down to the river. The man thought the Buddha was going to perform some sort of ablution or baptism, but the Buddha grasped him by the throat and thrust him under the water and held him there. Finally the man under the water thought, this is the end of it. When Buddha let him get up, he asked the man, when you were under the water what did you want the most? The man said, I wanted air. Buddha said, when you want salvation that much, then it shall be yours.

**MARY**  There is a great truth there. Truly, if you want this path and you want to make your way and prove it, you become almost desireless where your self is concerned, and you enlarge your vision.

**ANDREW**  It seems to me that there is a good suffering that happens when you suddenly get a glimpse of what can be. When you've gotten it from you night work, then you come forward and you are given this glimpse, and I don't think you're given it until you're ready for it, and when you compare it to what you are, it's such a contrast that it causes you to suffer. It causes you to suffer in a good way that you're willing to change.

**MARY**  We really come to a place where we see our soul. When we glimpse it, we want to be like that. That's simple talk. There's so many ways of expressing it, but you in your own way know that we do not live up to what we expect of ourselves.

**MARGARET**  It's partly because we haven't time.

**MIRIAM WILLIS**  And this would be true whether we were going there from Earth or if we had passed through death to the Afterlife.

**MARY**  The Temple of Retribution is a place where wrongs are made right. It's necessary to make visitations to this Temple at various times and from other levels of Planes. Here, man is shown how he can make amends to those he has neglected or wronged. Often one must go again and again to discover the ways and means of accomplishing this. Here we see the necessity of fulfilling this great Law, and we are given power to create ways and means of making such retribution as needed for our peace of mind and our ongoing in growth.

**MIRIAM WILLIS**  He may compensate by doing for another that which he neglected when on Earth.

**MARY**  If one has a dream that bothers them, that dream should be taken out to be understood. Many times it's an unfulfilled desire that runs along a person's life over and over again. They might even fasten it to someone they didn't want to be with, like I can't think of that person without having that dream. You yourself are the creator of your dream, you are the creator of your conditions. You anticipate difficulties in that person. The chemistry of that person and yourself is not in harmony.

So try to remember. That person may be on the Other Side. If you have it strongly enough in your mind and you write it out, we believe that they will receive that message. I know people who have entered my classes who have looked through their life and picked up the people they were not fond of and had differences with; they laid claim to forgiveness and life began to clear for them and they were different human beings. It was like lifting a burden from their shoulders. For we go burdened with dislikes. It's a false idea to think we just shed it because we do not. There's no display about it, there's no confessional, but to our souls we're confessing that through our stubborn ego we have wounded somebody.

We go over there. The debts we leave behind us, we pay over there. Don't ever forget that. I tell you all the beauty that's there, but don't forget that statement I bring you, that you need to recognize your indebtedness, especially if you have forgotten someone.

**ANDREW**  There are many Temples of Remembrance on different planes, but we learned that this particular one on the 2$^{nd}$ Plane we're asked to remember.

**MIRIAM WILLIS**  We're shown where we've forgotten to be thankful. There's a record room for past lives. God will help you to discover the fault you're supposed to overcome.

**LOLA**  I remember being there, in the Temple of Remembrance, in our night work. I recall this temple has opalescent walls, and walking there, you see the shadow of yourself, you recognize spots in need of correction, and you ask a teacher what they are.

**MARGARET**  I too brought back something from this Temple of Remembrance. I was permitted to see, as in a moving picture, the causes of imbalance of things forgotten or taken for granted or omitted through lack of gratitude or awareness, and also things I tried in the past to escape from. I felt the desire to do something about these neglects.

**MARY**  We also see the positive side of our lives, our kindnesses, self sacrifice, our generosity.

**HELEN MARSH**  I have something from the Temple of Revelation. This temple aims at greater spiritual enlightenment. When you're taken here, you read the record of the gifts you've been given and those you've accepted. Seeing the balancing forces of faith, endurance, patience and sincerity, you know where fault lies. It's within yourself, grounded on fear that there won't be enough, fear of not being able to reach your goal, fear of being able to survive in your old age. Yet we do have enough, and there is much to be thankful for each day if we can live in that consciousness.

**MIRIAM ALBPLANALP**  In the Temples of Revelation, you learn a great deal about yourself.

**MIRIAM WILLIS**  You surely do, and that causes one to seek further, don't you think? Shall we consider next the Temple of Worship, Mary?

**MARY** The 2nd Plane Temple of Worship is on a promontory with many steps up which the seeker climbs. One may turn back on a platform at each of twelve steps if he doesn't wish to go on up to the Temple. At each platform there are paths to the right and to the left, which lead to the places of desire where further attainment awaits. The Temple of Worship, vast and lovely in majestic grandeur, offers to the seeker a review of his week, his thoughts, words and deeds, opportunities well met and omissions that have retarded growth, as well as indulgences and prides that weaken, also selfless good that heals and advances the soul's growth. All is accounted for here, and one goes forth cleansed and healed seeing his true worth. He is free to worship the great Creator in expanded consciousness, strengthened to meet the pressures of life.

The Temple is of stone shining with an opalescent light and studded with precious stones. There are many sections and corridors that lead to rooms of cleansing and revealing. In worship there, one is renewed for the week to come. The week just ended is revealed and one is lifted in power of renewed faith and love.

**MIRIAM WILLIS** This is the first Temple of Worship we visit. Temples of Worship go up on many of the higher planes as well. Here, when we place on the altar the past week's record, this in turn comes back to us on our own vibration of merit or check, which holds within it the admonition not to repeat. At times we're surprised by unexpected, unrealized merit, or shocked by awareness of weaknesses, backsliding or failure. We need to rise into the high tower of spiritual consciousness and let the pure air of spirit sweep away the cobwebs of unreality.

**MARGARET** When we ask to be taken there, we're told to wrap ourselves in a soft blue light just before sleep.

**MIRIAM WILLIS** Violet has something to bring us, Mary.

**VIOLET** We entered the Temple of Worship and went down the right side through vaulted corridors. That which had not been visible now became so, as though some new and strange light had been cast upon the scene. All about us, as we stood in a group, were shimmering fibers of light that glistened and seemed to connect. They were like lovely spider webs or beads attached to the wall of the temple, then spreading outward, expanding like a sheet so that every part was connected with every other part by these sheets of threads, like an outer covering or transparent wall. What were these and what was their meaning? It made this temple quite different from any other we had seen. In this fragile outer sheet were lovely colors and tones.

I suspected they carried a special kind of power, one with a high voltage frequency and superlative force. They must be very full of specialized flow. These rays of power were in response to dedication to a source far greater than the little self, in response to surrender of that little self and its absorption into the greater-than-self, the divine. We were seeing presented to us answered prayer, its powerful force in operation to sanctify, cleanse and heal. A soft orange light envelops us, bringing a realization facing things in our lives that need development. We are not told where we're going, but our line moves off to another place where we meet a teacher who might quiz us about the last temple we were in and what was learned there.

The calmness of true worship is full of majestic power, a fusing of beauty and harmony in balanced proportion, rhythmic in music and color, as though for that moment in eternity one blended into the divine order. One is lifted and becomes a part of the whole, an instrument in the orchestra of the universal. Groups of people marching in sing songs of praise. They sing the songs of their ages of worship, each giving forth peons of praise, their devotion to the embodiment of divinity as they knew and realized it. Now the entire congregation joins in to form one choir accompanied by resounding organ music. At last the chord dies away, there is a stillness more impressive even than the sound, because now reverberates the immense power of cumulative worship, and we feel that it has reached the throne of God. From that throne we are now receiving his grace, severally given to each soul, an outpouring of life itself, God's gift to his entire creation.

**MARY**  Thank you, Violet.

**MARGARET**  I received an impression of an altar with white drape across the top. A purple front cover came down and went over the floor in front of it. There were crystal vessels on the altar and a crystal and ruby lighted something behind it.

**MARY**   That's in the 4th nave of the Temple of Worship. You'd better bring back more about it. You started out with a good description.

**ESTHER BARNES**   Mary, is the lotus very prominent in the Temple of Receptivity?

**MARY**   From now on in our night work, it is. Christian and Hindu alike accept the Temples because of the growth that takes place, the determination, and the divine progression of the soul.

**KATHY**   I saw lotuses larger than many people.

**MARY**   Oh yes. That is true, Kathy.

**KATHY**   One looked like it was a huge lamp; it was glowing with life--nothing but light.

**GERTRUDE**   We have special treatments in the Realization temples and areas too, don't we?

**MIRIAM WILLIS**   That's right. The Temple of Realization presents the soul's dawning and deepening realization of his Creator.

**MARY**   Subservient to all else that is realized is the consciousness of the inner presence, that which gives purpose to life, and a sense of security and rightness—for there is the Great One who has all the answers; sees all in divine perspective; knows the means and the end, the qualities within each soul and their possibilities.

**MIRIAM WILLIS**   The seeker frequents these areas many times to recall and experience the teaching given there, which helps to balance his forces, to empower and clarify his revelations, and cleanses him.

**MARY**   Here we learn the all-encompassing truth of the two great commandments given by Jesus: to love God with all one's heart, soul, mind and strength, and to love one's neighbor as oneself. One is especially impressed with the necessity of applying these commandments to all the details of his daily living.

The seeker seems to come to the end of himself; the very depths and heights of his being are explored with a poignancy of reality which carries him into a labyrinth of darkness and light, of rich beauty and barren deserts where he faces defeats and victories. Throughout, there is a theme of constant desire and of hunger and thirst to continue. One experiences the whole gamut of his inner life, though he has not journeyed forth nor moved from his place in a great antechamber. As a weariness possesses him, there immediately appears before him refreshing nectars and a couch supporting him that glows with rose amber rays of strength, which renews and infills his soul with peace. The seeker rises, poised and balanced in a great stillness of bliss beyond words, as though his entire life had been swept clean. He hungers not; his thirst is quenched, and he is expectant, knowing there is much still to be experienced that requires all his balanced forces in surrender.

**MIRIAM WILLIS** All these areas are for the purpose of further clearing the consciousness of those who seek, a training field for progression in this new life.

**EVA** There's an Isle of Forgetting on the chart.

**MARY** Can someone tell me what the Isle of Forgetting is for?

**MIRIAM WILLIS** Well, many souls who go over have a great yearning for the Earth, and they must forget that earth pull to go forward, because if Earth clings to one's consciousness they can't progress, so it becomes an inhibiting factor. The Isle of Forgetting clears that, so that they're able to look forward instead of back and experience a greater contentment and advancement.

**MARY** The Area of Forgetting is an area of further cleansing, so that no ill-feeling remains. Grudges are forgotten. We release guilts completely and bask in peace. We're bathed in the blue lavender of the holding force of peace, in order that the quality of security and rest be built into our being. We live in the equilibrium of its balance.

**MARGARET** Can people here on Earth, through mistaken ideas of love, keep people on the Isle of Forgetting from making progress by excess grief?

**MARY** Yes, excess grief might do that. But there are hours that the grief isn't "on." And many people's grief is selfish.

**WOODIE** I read a story about a mother who lost a little boy about four years old. And she wept so much; then one night she had a dream. She dreamed she saw a long line of children. All of them had lighted candles except one little boy, her son. She approached him and asked, "Why isn't your candle lit?" And he said, "I have lighted it so often, but your tears have put it out."

**MARY** I have great respect for grief. But I believe that when we develop the spiritual body as a counterpart of our physical body, there's a natural spiritual understanding that comes to us, a sympathetic understanding. We may not say a word, but with meditative prayer we hold that person who's gone over to a broader understanding.

**MARY WERTI** I had an experience similar to what Woodie was talking about. My nephew drowned. He was 14 years old. He came to me during meditation and said he wanted to tell all the people who had prayed for him that "it's been so very difficult for me to go on to higher learning, because they have all cried too much."

**GRACE** I think this course is a great consolation. Those of us who've lost loved ones, we grieve, we miss them being here by our side, but this course helps us to know that our loved one isn't that separated from us.

**MARY** That's right. So we have a point here in grief. The point of grief when we forget ourselves and love another human being or a spiritual being greater than ourselves, we have made a point of record. Whatever is done in love comes back to us in many, many ways.

**VIOLET** Another great consolation is the ability to communicate with our loved ones, the cross-communication of their visitation to Earth and our meeting them on the Other Side at night. That is, when souls are developed enough that this can take place.

**MIRIAM WILLIS** The Area of the Teachers Analysis lies to the left. It's where teachers from higher planes analyze the conditions of a soul's desiring to go further in development. When one is ready, he is taken to the area of development.

**SYLVIA** How are we affected by the Field of Recovery?

**MARY** The Field of Recovery is where we build the powers needed for healing the wounds of self realization. In this area, we fully recognize the spiritual body. Many people have not believed in such, nor ever thought of living beyond death, and need to become adjusted to this continuance. It's not always easy and is often resented, so the circles of rehabilitation involve accepting, building and becoming able in power to advance to the next level.

**MIRIAM WILLIS** In the Area of Forgiving, we're cleansed from all lingering of resentment, criticism, self blame and self justification. One forgives and regains self respect, accepts self and brother in love and feels God's forgiveness wholly.

**VIOLET** Isn't the Halls of Learning one of the most important areas on the 2$^{nd}$ Plane?

**MARY** Indeed yes. Discarnate people who don't believe in God spend a great deal of time here. There are many brilliant minds living on the 2$^{nd}$ Plane.

**DORIS** You told me this is where my husband is, Mary, on the 2$^{nd}$ Plane. My husband was an atheist. And if I do say, he had quite a brilliant mind.

**MIRIAM WILLIS** The Archives of Learning are available to the seeker who wishes evidence to satisfy his curiosity in a myriad of ways.

**MARY** The Archives of Learning are found at the right side of both the 1$^{st}$ and 2$^{nd}$ Planes. A storehouse of knowledge, inspired by the source of all truth and manifested by the human race is preserved here, available to the seeker.

**SYLVIA** And the Hall of Judgment is where one is judged by teachers as to readiness to go to the next plane of growth, the 3$^{rd}$ Plane.

**MIRIAM WILLIS**  Just above the Temple of Worship on its left, right side of the chart, we have the Temple of Renunciation. Here we learn to lay aside encumbrances, to renounce those things that inhibit growth, to go beyond the limits of self-interest and self-love. These are the root of many entanglements from which we must free ourselves, and here we learn to see renunciation as real freedom.

**MARY**  It's where we're breaking old moulds and renouncing regrets. Our thought forms are revealed as our attention is lifted from the lower to the higher. We find we've been carrying around a burden that can be discarded, something we've taken pride in, used as a crutch, when relinquished, rebounds to higher spiritual development.

**MIRIAM WILLIS**  The Mount of Renunciation begins on the $2^{nd}$ Plane and goes up. This is the Tempter at the top of the Mount. Notice that it's near the Earth.

**MARY**  We climb the Mount of Renunciation many times, and we go to these various temples many times, including after we've developed further than the $2^{nd}$ Plane.

**HELEN MARSH**  A recall: I was standing inside a temple waiting my turn. I noticed the wall was curved, and around it was a seat with a back to it in the colors of lettuce green, a beautiful rose, and sapphire blue. As it was my turn to move up, I saw an angel leave.

**MARY**  I think you were being called. We usually are called that way. You were in the Temple of Remembrance. From there you went to Revelation. It's something that you've been asking yourself for quite some time. You've been trying to remember and trying to account for something that took place in your life that bothered you, and you wonder now why it bothered you so much. It was revealed to you last night through the mirrors—just the whole reaction as you would see in a movie. You'll recall it.

Quite a number of you have met up with doors lately. I noticed as you were going through these tests, you were asked have you entered an open door? Well, some of you said yes, you had seen the door open. Some said, I haven't entered it yet, should I when I come to it again? Kindly, they answered yes.

**PATTI**  Mary, you haven't spoken of the Area of Doctors.

**MARY**  I can speak on that. Physicians who go over there usually rest for awhile. They're tired even if they've been in retirement, so they welcome the chance to take it easy for a while. Those doctors I knew who were in my classes who've gone over have initially been less earnest about getting started practicing medicine as soon as they got over there; they just first wanted to enjoy some relaxation.

As they began to realize that to further their development they'd have to go into some sort of work again, most of them wanted to continue in the medical field, so they'll go to the different orders of doctors and apply. They have to be re-educated; there's another, different training to go through. They then look around and very quickly find work. They find wonderful hospitals, wonderful equipment, new things that we know nothing about. They're so anxious to send it back to Earth in some way. I've known many doctors who have received from that source of supply. It was quite some time before the world received the different remedies that were put through, but they came through.

**PATTI**  How many orders of doctors are there?

**MARY**  Quite a few. They work in different bands, St. Luke's, for instance. I can't tell you how many orders of St. Luke are on the borderland and in those orders. Doctors take their work every day for healing services and for healing the world. The Order of St. Luke is a healing order.

**MIRIAM WILLIS**  Our St. Luke was one of the greatest doctors of his times.

**PATTI**  Are the bands limited to doctors?

**MARY**  No, they're not. Just as here, there are all kinds of attendant personnel who assist the doctors who are part of the band as well.

**LOLA**  You mean like nurses, secretaries, orderlies, researchers, and that sort of thing?

**MARY** That's right.

**LOLA** We receive so much from this course and from you, Mary. As Grace said, those we really love who've passed on, we miss them, but this class gives us the assurance that we're not really separated, because we've had the opportunity to prove for ourselves that it really is, as you say, one world without end.

**MARY** I've said to you before that within me lies a contentment, a great area of happiness, a joy of fulfillment that tomorrow I know there is another world, and believe me, I expect to go there. I don't expect to be at the right hand of God. I expect to go to the level of consciousness where I stand tonight. I expect to go on expressing life as I'm expressing it now. I know my way, and it's worth finding out something about. Think on it and let God guide you to the pattern of your soul to the place where you do know of that next world.

If we can once incorporate within our consciousness the Plan of Life here, we would somehow get the concert of the Plan of Life there. This is the shadow world, and that is a world of organized order different than here on Earth, because they have entered the beauty of all order within itself. And so it picks up its own rhythm, as many times our own lives form a rhythm that we can follow. And so in the temples there, you feel that that life is so ordered that the music of the spheres travels right with you. As you walk through the gardens or into the woods, you hear the trees whispering to each other. They whisper here on earth, but we haven't time to listen. I think the miniature things that travel through the grasses have their own language, and we can hear them if we intently listen. Just so, I feel the voice of the Master must occur to us over and over again, but we cannot hear, because our physical ears are listening.

Therefore, this training is supposed to lift you out of the physical far enough that you become 4<sup>th</sup> dimensional people. And in doing so, you hear this voice, this voice of peace and contentment, serenity, comfort, and gladness—always. Once it has been given--even as old as Sanskrit, way back where Aramaic flowed freely to the hearts of mankind, they said if you ever hear the invisible voice, you will never forget it. One goes back and forth many times from left to right on these maps, or vice versa, getting power on one side to go back and learn or do tests on the other. What it takes is patience and reaching out, almost into the wilderness of man's not knowing, to bring back some of those truths, and being able in all respects to master them.

# CHAPTER SEVENTEEN
# THE MOUNT OF RENUNCIATION

**MARGARET**  Mary, about the Mount of Renunciation: does it take different shapes at different times? I saw a shape the other night that was different than I'd ever seen before. Are the shapes I see symbolic?

**MARY**  You nearly always have to build it, you know. The temples you work with have to be perfected and landscaped every time. But we'll say that as you go into the Mount of Renunciation, you realize there's something to overcome. You meet up with great beauty, but sometimes there's a corridor where the gate is locked. You haven't developed to the place in your physical life, you haven't the development to walk through that gate. And so you come back into a Hall of Remembrance or to the Temple of Forgiveness, and there's something way back, something you've done that has kept you from realizing all that you've been given. You've avoided responsibility and taken too much for granted. The Mount of Renunciation, also the Temple of Renunciation certainly do clean up the background of your life. And there's plenty of healing to do, for we have selfishly gone about our own way. So we see a picture before us at the Mount, of things that have affected other lives. We had no intention of doing what we did, but that's what happened.

And so, we're told how we can clear it up, and we go about it. It's nice if someone's living on Earth and you can go to them directly and say please forgive me, I didn't intend to handicap you or do the thing I did that hurt you. If you're aware of it and someone is living, I certainly would to that. It's a long time and hard labor over there on the Other Side to undo some of the things that you've done on Earth, and it's even harder after you go over there as a permanent resident, to be able to find those people and ask their forgiveness. Forgiveness is a law between yourself and God. And "even as you have done it unto the least of these, you have done it unto me" is one of the laws.

**ANDREW**  It seems that a lot of things take longer to get done over there. You've told us that we can accomplish in five years on Earth what it would take twenty years to do on the Other Side.

**MARY** That's why it's so important to do all you can with this life, while you're here.

**MIRIAM WILLIS** And that's why this teaching is so valuable.

**MARGARET** It isn't clear to me how the ideal will match the Mount of Renunciation.

**MARY** The Mount requires certain things of you, and your ideal has to undo what is against the path to the Mount. If we've wronged someone and we have been "so right" within ourselves, why go to the Mount? You can't go any higher until you do something about it within yourself. If I had taken money from someone and couldn't repay it because the person was no longer living, I might give money to someone else who needs, and pay that debt. In other words, we're responsible for the debts we owe. Many times there would be no way to repay directly; maybe the person himself didn't know what he'd done, but that's the thing we're facing over there.

**CONNIE** Would the Mount of Renunciation be different for each person?

**MARY** Oh, of course. Now for instance, you could say I live a simple life and honors have been few. All right, then take someone who went the whole way, they tasted of the greatest that man could offer. Someone else may have deserved the plum that was handed to that person. So the person is responsible to that person he took from. Let's take the person who borrowed from friends and relatives, goes bankrupt and can't pay them back. He should have known better, his friends say. Now he owes those people.

**KATHY** A friend of mine the other day mentioned a dream she had. She was with her husband and children; they were climbing up a mountain in a dark area and came to a lighted place with beautiful trees and a serene pool. A woman in a particular house said, "This little girl stays here; you go on to the next place." This had a quality of the numinous and seemed like a real experience to my friend.

**MARY** I would say she was introduced to the Mount of Renunciation, which a very rugged thing to start with. It takes courage to start climbing. A mountain climber will at first be very active; then he comes to a rough spot and stops. Everyone who has started up the Mount of Renunciation has said, I wonder why I started. You are so tested by dispositional traits once you start climbing this Mount. It means leaving behind us all the things we have wrongly used as our own. We have claimed the use of things that didn't belong to us, because most of the traits we had that did belong to us are not so acceptable. I'm speaking of those uncouth things that are inside of us that we need to get rid of.

**MARGARET** Isn't it the Mount of Renunciation that keeps holding us back? Because we can't give up what we keep clinging to, because it's embedded in our ego and we can't release it?

**MARY** You're right. That Mount of Renunciation is like Christ's 40 Days, because you do renounce the things that you desire most. Very few people accomplish the Mount of Renunciation in a short time. It takes about the 20$^{th}$ plane to stand on top and wave back. But you do get up a good ways and on various plateaus; you find you bring back certain dreams and experiences that all men have had throughout the ages. So that's proof you've climbed that Mount of Renunciation to a certain degree. Christ went 40 degrees up that mountain; he was at the top and he stayed there 40 days. No other being we have heard of has been able to do that.

In his message back to us, his idea was if we could even climb ten paces and be sure of ourselves, we would have entered a highly spiritual vibration. Christ said to the disciples, if you could come up the Mount with me ten paces and not go backward, if you're looking up and I'm beckoning to you, no matter where I am, Heaven or Earth, if I'm beckoning to you, mount the next paces and see that you don't fall. So then they mounted the next ten paces, and they were able to kneel. That's when they started the healing.

There was quite a company of his people that became healers, more than are entered into our Bible. Documents say our Christ had eighty followers, not just the twelve disciples. It was quite a task to feed them. And there are some accounts that he had over three hundred followers.

**MIRIAM WILLIS** And he took them all up the Mount of Renunciation.

# CHAPTER EIGHTEEN
# THE ANIMAL KINGDOM
# AND MORE CLASS QUESTIONS

**ESTHER ESTABROOK**  I recall that one evening, you spoke of the Animal Kingdom. Where is it?

**MARY**  It's on the 2nd Plane, although we haven't put it on the charts.

**EMILY**  Why not?

**MIRIAM WILLIS**  Because we're mainly concerned with humans here! As people, we have enough to think of!

**JEANNE**  Mary, the animals, do they ever come out of the Animal Kingdom? If we dream about a horse ... I know that's supposed to mean spiritual power, but could we actually see a horse in a temple?

**MARY**  No, they would not be in the temples. No animal would ever be.

**JEANNE**  Not even on special occasions?

**MARY**  No, I don't think so, dear. You would have to go to the 2nd Plane to be near the area of the Animal Kingdom.

**MIRIAM ALBPLANALP**  A dream of a horse would be a symbol of power, wouldn't it, Mary?

**MARY**  It would be symbolism. Horses are strength, spiritual power, yes. And we see them because they're a symbol of Earth. They have served man in the most powerful ways for many years, have they not? Because you can direct the horse. You couldn't direct the ox, which may be stronger, but can't be directed. So there are other animals that have more strength, but they don't have the intelligence, or they don't have what God gave the horse to understand man's demands upon them.

**MIRIAM WILLIS**  And the old mules. You know they're strong, and they have a great deal of endurance, but you know they back right up.

**MARY** Now I can add one thing to that. It is an historical fact that all the great churches, the cathedrals where they hold the activities and the feast days and the blessing of the animals, they invite the saints to come and work in this festival. And many a priest in the old days would write in his memoirs of the wonderful saints that came, and how the animal gave – the cow gave more milk, the goat gave forth a great amount after that blessing. And that is what we have seen down through the ages.

**SYLVIA** So we know that animals are susceptible to spiritual vibrations.

**WOODIE.** Am I to understand then, that our pets do go on to another life?

**MARY** Oh, yes. There's the Animal Kingdom where they dwell!

**PATTI** Some weeks ago you were talking to us about animals, and you said that there were some people who would not meditate if there was a cat in the room. What was the reason for that?

**MARY** Well, if you could see a cat's aura, it is sparking continually. It comes from the wild animal. The domestic cat is from the wild cat family, and it's in eternal movement. And then it becomes so very, very quiet. That's why the Hindu goes apart and sits a long time alone, because he doesn't want the interference of animal or man. And there's that law among different religious sects where a cat can't be in a room where meditation is going on.

**JEANNE** Is it possible a person could reach a point where a cat wouldn't disturb them?

**MIRIAM WILLIS** It's a matter of disturbed vibration, then, isn't it?

**MARY** Yes, it is. Now, a cat's vibration is very much swifter than a dog's. It's almost a racing vibration. A cat will take a leap from your lap and go to the door in no time at all. A dog gets up and stretches, and you know what the dog is going to do, so you wouldn't be startled by anything.

**JEANNE** I was wondering if it was the nervousness about anticipating being startled.

**LOLA** I thought of that, Jeanne.

**BILL JACKSON** I think there are those among us who learn to meditate under all kinds of conditions. Clara and I have two young children who can distract us more than our cats would. It's been challenging, but we've learned to adjust and it's been good training for us.

**JEANNE** What about a horse's vibration?

**MARY** It's the highest vibration in the animal kingdom. According to the history that I've been given, a horse is the cleanest animal that lives. It doesn't bury its food; it doesn't steal food; it can be hitched to a post and try to eat; it will eat right up to the bark of a tree, but then it ceases, and it would die if someone didn't unbridle it. These are some of the things that have been given.

**LINDA** Why, in Egypt, such a devotional culture, did they worship cats?

**MARY** The cat was a great defense. People had such fear of the cat. The temple cat was, like we would say to a dog, go get it! They were so trained. And that was because they would go into the forest, the wilds, and bring a cat and train it. And it had enough of its wildness in it that it could scratch, and it usually jumped for the face of a person. And they were extremely strong in their front paws ... the temple cats.

**GLENN** Man can learn a lot from animals. In some ways, they're more evolved than we are.

**MARY** I've told you before and I'll tell you again, do unto others as you would they do unto you was the Law of God's people from the beginning. Among the animals you'll find that law being lived many times, in peace. A mother lioness will save the other lioness's cub, nestle it and nurse it. That's the law of doing unto others. And that is the most powerful that God has expressed. Altogether, until man entered Africa, animals drank at the same water hole; they took turns. And then man went in to take them away as living specimens. And out of that, they began to fight, even fight each other.

So we are the intelligent ones. As God breathed into us the breath of life, he breathed into us this intelligence that's greater than the animal, and asks us to recognize it. Because within the soul is that plan of life for us that would make us truly great people. But life is so complicated. We've grown into patterns of living that seem almost impossible to change.

**NOTE**: My first book in this series *Planes of the Heavenworld*, Chapter Sixteen, gives further information about the Animal Kingdom, and is included at the back of this book.

**FRANK** When I'm sitting quietly in meditation, I get blocked by having to stop and clarify what I see from the intellectual viewpoint. When we're sitting here consciously thinking we're in this consciousness, does a part of us go on higher, even though we're not aware of it?

**MARY** You're unaware because you're not aware of using that spiritual body. How many of us have been higher up? How much of the upstairs of our mind have we used? That's one of the things you want to think about. When we go into the Channel, we go upstairs. Each one of you has your own accumulation of spiritual knowledge. When your spiritual eyes and spiritual ears are opened, you can read the knowledge of your spirit. We have five spiritual senses and five physical senses. They are the ten talents. Christ gave you the cleanest and clearest picture of the man who used his talents and the man who didn't.

**ANDREW** The wise and foolish virgins.

**MARY** Yes. To me, the Color Channel is the safest way of having spiritual experiences and finding the spiritual knowledge of our talents.

**GENE** I was wondering, what about people who aren't fortunate to have a class like this, people who never become seekers, and end up going no farther than the 2nd or 3rd Plane when they graduate from Earth?

**MARY** They have a belief. There are very few people that haven't a belief. It's sometimes the intellectuals who haven't had the faith to believe there's a beyond or a Heaven World; they don't believe in the ongoing of life; it's just "when I 'm dead I 'm dead." And they get over there and they stay on the 2nd Plane. They haven't sinned against the Law of Creation – sin is the only word I know how to use. But anyway, they haven't wronged anyone to the extent of murder, extreme cruelty, or something of the kind, so they're not placed in the Magnetic Field, but they're placed along with the bigots. And I think it's quite a trial to live there. Some of them move out.

**EVELYN**   Since not every atheist is a bigot, it must be a difficult for some atheists to live alongside people who are bigots. Maybe these two types are placed together for a reason.

**HANK**   Pardon this theological question. Do you see the importance of the insistence that people make the decision for Christ before they pass on?

**MARY**   No. You either love Christ in this life or you don't. That eleventh hour redemption comes from our religious denominations. It's probably fine that you've accepted, but think of the dear man that never knew Christ in other nations, other cultures, other traditions.

**GENE**   We're not to judge others. It's almost impossible not to, in case of atrocities.

**MARY**   Everybody needs to judge atrocities. And no one can read the headlines without having feelings. I would try to imbue the world with something more decent than what is written up in the headlines. Many times we're setting a judgment on something we know so little about. I think just use discretion. Because you yourself are the result of your own thinking; a man is what he thinks.

**JEANNE**   I asked a question in Tuesday color class, and it was decided maybe it was something to ask again Friday night, so I thought maybe I might ask you. There've been some people who've said it's not necessary to be asleep to go out at night after you come to take us, that we go even if we're awake in meditation, but you said "no." Which is it? I meant could they be in meditation and still go out, or would they definitely have to be asleep?

**LOLA**   I was wondering the same thing. Yesterday afternoon I had two hour nap, which is unusual, and I had a feeling like I often do in the morning as I come back, of an awareness of something, but I didn't catch it.

**MARY**  I would have to say this way. Mary Weddell, your teacher, did not take you out, but a Teacher from the Other Side. You have an unfinished piece of work, or you had to say something, and they picked you up at that time of induced sleep, to show you something that you needed to know, something in your life that had gone wrong.

**JEANNE**  And if they were in meditation instead of asleep?

**MARY**  If they were in meditation instead of asleep I would say this: that they would wait until they dropped asleep, and then they would be picked up. They have to be in that vibration of sleep, and certainly meditation and prayer makes it easier for me to handle them, for they are then, partially, in that world.

**JEANNE**  You know the expression "an independent." Miriam used that one Tuesday – a person who could take themselves out to the temples. Would that person have to be a master?

**MARY**  I would say that person had to be a 20th Plane person, if they did it, and I wouldn't know whether they were masters or not; that's something they would have to decide on the Other Side.

**SANDRA**  I'd like to ask about those on the astral plane who are earthbound. We're told that some people when they so called die, stick around the Earth.

**MARY**  At first they do not stay around. Like everyone else, they're met by their loved ones. Even though their consciousness has been asleep on Earth, they have this period in which everything is right. They're resting in the midstream of God consciousness while they're in Restland. After those seven days, they move into an area where their former consciousness takes hold.

**PATTI**  You said many people want to come back to Earth; that's their greatest desire.

**MARY**  Earthbound and that aren't the same thing. Earthbound souls are those that had been in sin and suffering and are bound to Earth through habit.

**LOLA**  There must be colors that protect a person from being intruded on by earthbound people.

**MARY**  The Channel is your protection. By going through the Channel, we are walking along with people of one mind. The colors are a protection.

**GENE**  The people who are lost over there, wandering around in this nether region, are they people who were exposed to the seven days of love?

**MARY**  Every one of them had that chance, and they still know it. They're told when they go to the Hall of Examiners and go on to the doctors, through their intelligence they could have worked it out. They know all the reasons why. Then they're sent to one of the lower planes. They were also told there are schools and temples there that will accept then, and that they can come back up, and there will always be teachers who will be glad to receive them. After they go through that Examining Field, they nearly always know where they're going.

**ROWENA**  We're trained over there to give back to humanity in any way that fits our abilities. What about a person who fails to recognize they have, for instance, healing ability?

**MARY**  Well, now we assist the invisible helpers in a class over there. And if a person has healing power here on earth and fails to use it, at night you single that person out, if you're a teacher and you've seen it in the aura, and you say to the leader of a band of healers, "I have someone that can help." Then you're taken at night, maybe a short time, you're taken to where healing is needed, you add your bit.

**PATTI**  Could someone living on the Earth who trained as a nurse, for instance, could she go at night and perform duties as a nurse in a hospital in the Heaven World?

**MARY**  They might go with a group of Earth nurses where there's a disaster. If you have development you can do so through the force of your development. They're pleased to have Earth people to work back to Earth because of the natural vibration. Our knowledge of a disaster on Earth is more immediate, and you're more able to help people than you would be if you were someone who lived in the spirit world. That's one of the reasons the teachers are here, to train you to help.

**GRACE** Would you talk about what a tie-in is at night, when your energy or a person's energy is used for something at night.

**MARY** Here's an example. There was a person who was very close to us. She was in a train wreck. She thought for months afterwards how much she could have done for other people. But she didn't do anything. She just sat on the side of the road with people suffering all about her, and felt helpless. I said to her, maybe they didn't need you physically, maybe you were tied in spiritually. A person walking around trying to help somebody with broken bones or otherwise, they listen very little to a person like that. If there are invisible helpers around and a person is sitting there praying, holding power, they pick up that energy, and that's what I call a tie in. Creative energy that you sit there, holding, belongs to God, and belongs to every other person. It's transferable that way, when a person is one-pointed in their wishing to help.

**LENORE** Can you be used in your night work for the same sort of thing?

**MARY** Yes.

**LORNA** I get frequent vivid fleeting impressions, especially upon waking, and also when I'm playing the piano. I wonder if these could all be combined, if I could make sense of a particular theme that way, by putting several of these impressions or pictures together.

**MARY** Just write it down and add to it. One of these days, it will fit into the symbology of the temple. For that's how we grow, not by long strides but by a step at a time. That growth is a secure growth. If it's made daily, we're sure of it, just as surely as light to the darkness.

**ESTHER BARNES** I'd like to mention that most of us work during the day at stressful jobs, so our daytime hours are full of emotional challenges. If this weren't the case, we'd be leading much more peaceful lives.

**MIRIAM WILLIS**  And credit is given us for every day we've been under strain. So few people can live without stress; we're so merged into the lives of other people.

**MARY**  Few people live exemplary lives every day, but somewhere in every day there's a highlight that God himself can approve of. What we have to think about is to prolong the length of the highlights of the day. I'm telling you that eternal lives are built on our small blessings.

**GENE**  It interests me that different groups, seekers from other cultures and of other beliefs, also go to the Other Side at night, and that there are teachers from diverse disciplines working with them.

**MARY**  There are plenty of Buddhist monks there who are going into the midst of the horrors of the nether world, working. We see them when they come to the temples for worship. There's a place for them the same as there's a place for everyone. Many of them are still on this side of life, but they work over there at night and their work is magnificent. They are entirely removed from the world. They're seemingly ageless, there's nothing they can't do, and in such long stretches of time. I'm speaking of a living Buddhist, one of the monks, maybe one of those that are working in their own home, and at night they work as a teacher over there as I work. And the depths to which they go without trepidation to pick up someone they think can be saved for the Kingdom!

They're wonderful in that they are on their own lines. That's going to raise a question. There's a line of demarcation between the different nations as their people come over; yet it's all one line. That's the law of love that operates in God's kingdom. And each person, wherever they happen to be, is sought and given the chance to reveal their desires and go to higher realms. Just as surely as they wish, it will be given them. It happens both ways, whether the decision is to go up or to go down.

**KATIE**  I'd like to clarify what you've said about asking for help. How could you tell, if you're trying to live by inner guidance, whether you're asking for outside assistance?

**MARY**  I think anyone who prays for assistance gets it. If you ask, ask with faith that you're going to receive. Know it's for you before you ask. Make it truly yours.

**JOHN #1**  Many times you go into the Channel and up to the Fount of Supply, the height of consciousness, and you offer your prayer there.

**MARY**  The fulfillment can come through the Channel; that's right.

**MIRIAM ALBPLANALP**  You've said each problem goes in pairs. If you escape part, that part will come back and hit you. Could you give an example of the two halves of the problem?

**MARY**  If there's something we have to face, it will repeat itself again and again until we accept it. One half of the problem is rejection and the other half is acceptance. You weren't alerted to the fact that you'd made a mistake. I could say it in a dozen ways in my life. If I resented answering something, if I resented having to take on something, it came again and I had to face it. Any problem that belongs to you will repeat itself until you accept the responsibility. Most of us don't like having to face responsibility. Responsibilities are the causes of side stepping and getting ourselves into difficulties later. You accept when you reach out, identify yourself with the problem, and take care of it as nearly as you can. If a person wants to pay a debt, recognition is the thing they have to make. But it's something that belongs to you and no one else.

**MARGARET**  When we're conscious of the fact we've failed to do something, instead of having to wait and have the thing that we have to answer for come up ten years later, how can we make that up now?

**MARY**  This is how we can go about it. Try to pick up somewhere, someone in our consciousness and say, I've repaid that debt. If you can't repay it to the individual themselves, repay it to someone else. You'll find that it's cleansed. Become conscious of your lack of realization, of your need. The strange thing is, we've come down right through the ages with love ye one another and love thy brother as thyself, which no one has manifested but the Christ. But in becoming reconciled to ourselves, we have great charity toward the other person. We don't see just the ugly things about that person or the things we dislike. It's a good plan to look at the eyes of that person — the windows of the soul — and if that person responds with a smile, that's your starting point.

The smile between you is a look of recognition between two souls that sometime or other will meet again. I believe that those who've had the hardest time in getting along with people here on Earth will meet them in Heaven. We will probably see all the things where we were wrong and they were wrong and these things will be cleared. I believe the path we take each night is the clearing house of our souls, and we don't need to awaken the next morning with any feeling of guilt. For every day is one day to live again, and to live anew, not in the dregs of the past.

A man on the Path of Light who is truly converted cannot get off the Path. The light within us is the Path. If we live the Path, life is eased for us; we don't strive quite so hard to get something that overreaches our destination. Sometimes a simple thing will build you into a greater person. One of the questions posed in these temples is what was I commissioned to do upon the Earth? What we're seeking in the enlightened soul is a pearl of great price. No man can have it unless he develops the casket to carry it. And within us is this natural place for carrying God's love and emulating the life of Christ. So as travelers along the way, we know enlightenment only comes on the even keel of a good disposition and letting your fellow man live as you would want to live. By attaining the truth of yourself, overcoming heavy emotions, using the Color Channel, you enter your world each day prepared to meet all the trials that come your way.

There is a sense of something greater than ourselves, an inner presence which in our quietest moments is more perceptible than in the turmoil of the world, something that enfolds our entire being. What we call the spirit in man stretches to something supreme, which is simply man's search for God. God's answer is the development of man's soul. In your search for self mastery, you come to recognize your own divine spirit. For your real world is invisible, the world of your spiritual life within. The place you now stand, you have reached through listening and following an invisible path, an adventure through faith.

**LOLA** . Faith stands with us in this life and in the Afterlife. We never lose what we've gained.

**GENE** I'm interested to know about the invisibles, who one hears are there with us as we're ready to leave this world for the next.

**MIRIAM WILLIS**   When a patient is close to experiencing the transition of death, often medical personnel in hospitals will tell you they see invisibles from the Other Side hovering around the bed, a sign that the patient will soon pass.

**MARY**   When I was much younger, probably around twenty-five, I was standing near the hospital bed of a dear friend, and I noticed the strangest thing. It was as if something was forming all around the person. I would say it was rather like a cloud, a sort of vaporizing material that seemed fog-like. It lessened, it got lighter and lighter. I went out in the corridor and asked an intern who was passing down the hall to come to the room. He thanked me for calling him, because, he said, 'That person is passing out.' Since then, many times I've sat at the bedside and waited for people to pass. And I always felt happy that I could be there, because I knew the way. I believe in learning the way of life and the way of death. It is one life eternal. If we could accept that and translate it to our inner selves, we would live in immortality now. At least a part of the time we would live away from the world's hardships. If we could just help someone who was ready to die to know, to teach them something of immortality, we would have done a great service.

**CONNIE**   We had a reading that was called *Overture*, about the passage of the soul to heaven, and I was wondering, when does 'Overture' usually end for most people?

**MARY**   I think it ends with their delight in being in that radiant land, I think when the storms of life move away from them. It's like a still sea at that time. And I have been told it lasts just as long as they will carry it with them, not worry about the known and the unknown, when they once settle back, forget the drama of life, and then sit within that. That is theirs, and they have found peace. I have known people who have found such beautiful peace! And what they said to me: 'Oh Mary, won't you just talk for me and let me tell the world?'

######

## ABOUT THE AUTHOR

Jeanne Rejaunier graduated from Vassar College, Poughkeepsie, New York, and did postgraduate studies at the Sorbonne, Paris, the Universities of Florence and Pisa, Italy, the Goetheschule, Rome, and at UCLA. While a student at Vassar, she began a career as a professional model and subsequently became an actress in Manhattan, Hollywood and Europe, appearing on and off Broadway, in films and television, on magazine covers internationally and as the principal in dozens of network television commercials.

Jeanne achieved international success with the publication of her first novel, *The Beauty Trap*, which sold over one million copies and became Simon and Schuster's fourth best seller of the year, the film rights to which were purchased outright by Avco-Embassy. Jeanne has publicized her books in national and international tours on three continents in five languages. Her writing has been extolled in feature stories in *Life, Playboy, Mademoiselle, Seventeen, BusinessWeek, Fashion Weekly, Women's Wear, W, McCalls, American Homemaker, Parade, Let's Live, Marie-Claire, Epoca, Tempo, Sogno, Cine-Tipo,* the *New York Times,* the *Los Angeles Times*, and countless other publications.

In addition to *The Beauty Trap*, Jeanne published novels *Odalisque at the Spa, The Motion and the Act, Affair in Rome,* and *Mob Sisters,* as well as nonfiction titles *Planes of the Heavenworld, My Sundays with Henry Miller; The 50 Best Careers in Modeling, Modeling From the Ground Up, Runway to Success, The Video Jungle, Astrology and Your Sex Life, Astrology For Lovers, Japan's Hidden Face, The Complete Idiot's Guide to Food Allergy,* and *The Complete Idiot's Guide to Migraines and Other Headaches.*

Branching out as a filmmaker, Jeanne produced, directed, filmed, and edited the four hour documentary, *The Spirit of '56: Meetings with Remarkable Women.*

######

## CHAPTERS FROM PLANES OF THE HEAVENWORLD
by Jeanne Rejaunier

### Chapter Two – Meeting Mary

As I continued my studies in Miriam's Tuesday group, I was full of questions that only being a part of Mary's Planes class could satisfy. After a few months of faithful attendance studying color, I was finally invited to my first Friday class. My excitement mounted as Carmen, George and I were on our way to Pasadena. Of course, our conversation centered on the Planes.

I had learned more about the Planes in preparation for my participation in the classes. Echoing what had been said in the Tuesday night group, Carmen and George emphasized the inter-relatedness of our two worlds and the fact that the night teaching had been around for thousands of years. George, who was an opera fan, noted that, "Mozart's *The Magic Flute* even highlights one of the temples. Mozart was an initiate, he was a Mason, as was his librettist. The Temple of Wisdom is an important part of that opera."

"Yes, it's central to it," I agreed, being an opera fan myself.

George continued, "E flat major is the central key throughout the opera, beginning with the overture. E flat major has a special significance in Masonry. One reason is that the key of E flat major is written with three flats, which is symbolic of the Trinity. Mozart begins the opera's overture using three trombones, symbols of the Higher Self, and throughout the opera, fanfares, chords played by those three trombones, announce the temple initiations. *The Magic Flute* is an opera about spiritual initiation in the Temple of Wisdom."

Carmen said, "Mary has taken us to the Temple of Wisdom in our nightwork, along with our other temples."

George added, "Music and color are interrelated. When Mary plays the organ or piano, she sees colors emanating from her hands that are the colors of the notes she's playing. Color and music are heightened when we visit the Planes."

To provide an overall design of the Other Side, Mary had created detailed charts, drawn by Miriam, showing some of the manifold areas of consciousness in the Heavenworld. Carmen had shown me xerox copies of some of the charts the class had covered thus far in its Planes study. I saw that all the heavenly Planes incorporated, in addition to their numerous temples, features such as towers, mounts, plateaus, power stations and power houses, power lines and power centers, rhythmic centers, spirals, supply stations, libraries, retreats, islands, archives, vortexes, vistas, plains, seas, cities of light, and more. All of these existed on the etheric Planes that we would not only inhabit after death, but that the class was privileged to visit nightly in their present lives, thanks to Mary.

The class study was up to the 5th Plane, having already covered the lower planes, which, according to the Carmen's charts, hosted regions in which, on the 3rd Plane, contained, in addition to halls of learning, private homes, churches, synagogues, mosques and other places of worship; Baby Land, Children's Land and the Children's Plateau; as well as the Temples of Realization, Remembrance, Revelation, and Thanksgiving.

A Plateau between the 3rd and 4th Planes contained the Field of Expanding Consciousness, the Area of Assembly and the Area of Creative Energy.

Moving upward, on the 4th Plane were located the Temples of Giving, Understanding, Creative Silence and Rhythm, Remembrance, Self Illumination, Healing Waters, Harmony, Heart, Bells, Reconciliation, and Music and Song. Mary's group had already assimilated teachings in all of the above, all of which preceded the 5th Plane, the temples of which the class was now visiting on a nightly basis, one temple per week.

"What happens in all these different temples?" I asked. "What type of teaching do you or did you receive there? How has it changed you?"

George was at the wheel, with Carmen sitting beside him in the passenger seat. Carmen twisted around to face me and stayed that way for the remainder of the drive. She said, "If you like, I'd be happy to share my notes and tapes with you, which should give you a good idea. I've taped all the Friday classes since I started with Mary."

George added, "Every week, we also a special receive written message from Mary, summarizing the inspired teaching the class has received that week in the temples visited each night. In addition to that, class members tell about their individual experiences on the Planes."

"Everyone on Earth shares the goal of soul evolution, whether they realize it or not," Carmen declared. "We humans reincarnate with the desire to evolve, and even when it seems we're not making progress, we really are, simply by undergoing life's experiences. We learn through hardship, failure and mistakes even more than through our successes and triumphs. And of course, you know what they say about an unexamined life. This is where the Planes studies really makes a difference, giving us accelerated learning and the means to accomplish it."

"Being with Mary as our teacher means we can do a great deal more spiritually than we could otherwise. Examining our lives is what we do a tremendous amount of at night," George said. "Each of us undergoes very personal experiences, which we bring back to our ordinary consciousness and incorporate in our lives."

"We New Age seekers are constantly working on ourselves, clearing out negative patterns," Carmen added. "I'm always asking what is life trying to teach me? Why am I having this experience? What lesson do I need to learn? And I'm given guidance in my nightwork."

"You'll have answers to a lot of your questions from tonight on, Jeanne," George assured me. "These classes are so special. Everyone is of similar mind, on a very high level. To paraphrase what Jesus said, when two or more people of similar vibration are gathered for a shared purpose, their combined energy is multiplied exponentially." George then amended his statement. "I think the exact quote is more like 'When two or more are gathered in my name, there shall I be among you.' And it's absolutely true. We all feel that in the class, a shared energy that increases and magnifies in intensity."

Carmen said, "There's such tremendous love shared between us in the classes, even though we only see one another for a couple of hours a week – a couple of earth hours, that is. But our strongest link is the one that binds us, our nightwork in the temples where Mary takes us."

George said, "The link between this life and the Afterlife becomes stronger and stronger as you progress in the Planes."

"When a person of faith dies, he can accept the transition into the next world as a natural process, a mere change in consciousness, like stepping from one room into another," Carmen added. "But for others, death may be traumatic. We see every night that there's nothing to fear about death, and everything to look forward to."

"Even if we have no fear," George said, "we need to be prepared for what lies ahead. Acknowledging the next step, what's beyond, and how we fit in there is important."

"Knowing that, we welcome the Afterlife," Carmen agreed, "seeing it's truly a magnificent chapter in our continual progress toward spiritual realization."

I asked Carmen again what type of experiences she'd had in the temples.

"I'll be telling the class about this one tonight. Relating our nightwork experiences is part of what we always do in class – share what happened to us the past week," Carmen said. "Last night, I had what's called a water test. I was immersed in a narrow enclosure the size and shape of a barrel. It was very dark green inside, containing water up to my head. Ordinarily I'd feel claustrophobic in this type of situation, but in this test, I didn't at all. I had no anxiety; to the contrary, I felt emboldened – brave and confident."

"And?"

"In terms of physical and emotional description, that's it. I shouldn't even use the word physical, because of course it's not physical at all, it's etheric – although it relates to physical existence, to something I needed to be aware of. These tests increase understanding and give energy for growth in the physical life."

"The testing sounds very interesting," I commented.

"It's not easy to describe to someone else, because each experience is so personal, it's uniquely yours. Only your own soul grasps the full message, the uplift, the release, the positive aspect of what you've been shown."

George said, "Sometimes we can pinpoint work over there, tests we go through, match them with things going on in our lives. Not always. But the energy is working whether we realize it or not."

It was nearly 7 pm. A hush enveloped the grounds as we drew up to the Pasadena house. All was quiet and peaceful as Carmen, George and I entered the airy front studio-meeting room, joining others who were already seated. The first thing I noticed was that the chairs were facing a different wall than on Tuesday. Tuesdays, the chairs were turned in a horizontal direction, whereas now, on Friday, they faced Miriam's stunning portrait of Jesus.

I already knew many of the students present from Tuesdays; others were new faces I would soon meet, not only in the Friday classes throughout my Pasadena years, but nightly on the Other Side for decades to come. I joined the rest of the group in pre-class meditation. Green bayberry candles emitted a pleasant, evocative aroma.

Miriam appeared from a side door to stand in front of the group, clad in a becoming silk dress in her keynote color of sky blue. She nodded to sixtyish, auburn-haired Grace, our Friday night organist, who struck the opening chords of one of the hymns from the SFF hymnal.

Through music, prayer, meditation, and the evoking the inner channel of the Keys of the Kingdom, the group's vibration was raised. To Grace's accompaniment, the class sang three hymns to build power in the room, preparing to receive our heavenly teachers. Traditionally, this phase would end with singing the hymn "The Garden of Prayer.

A quiet fullness descended upon the room as our group entered the silence. You could feel currents growing, mounting. Basking in the stillness, Miriam led us in guided meditation, beginning with "climbing the channel," inviting each of us to clothe ourselves in our keynote color. As of yet, I had not been given my own keynote or keynote color. That would come later. So I clothed myself in royal purple, the color of faith, to join Miriam and the others in climbing the Channel.

"We stand in the royal purple of Faith and mount to the grey lavender of the Holding Force of Patience; uplifted into the pink lavender of Inspiration, we travel into the rose lavender of the Spiritual Voice ... " Miriam began, ever full of conviction.

We each drew these colors to ourselves for a few seconds at a time, as, arms outstretched, receiving power, Miriam continued speaking firmly in her strong, commanding voice:

"... from the blue orchid of Prophesy, we cross the delicate yellow bridge of Enlightenment, which lifts us to the brilliant rose orchid of the Message Bearer, and on to the stunning red lilac of the Holding Force for the Band of Teachers, and once more, we cross a yellow Enlightenment bridge, arriving at the soft peach of Union of Mind and Spirit ... from the light blue orchid of Brotherhood we mount into the blush orchid of Serenity... and then, from the pale green bridge of Desirelessness onto the rose bisque of Grace, we come to the light blue lavender of Peace ... And now we stand at the Fount of Supply ..."

Each color gave uplift and support to the spiral above it. Because each succeeding color is of a higher vibration than the one below it, one "climbed" in consciousness while ascending the Channel. At the word "peace," the class partook of silence, resting in the quietude of lifted spirit in silent expectancy and communion with the Infinite. Along with everyone, I infilled my soul center, absorbing etheric colors at the Fount of Supply, gateway between the visible and invisible worlds, opening to super-consciousness, transcending the illusion of matter, rising into fourth dimensional consciousness, seeing the Unseen, "living in eternity now," where we become acutely aware of the oneness of our two worlds. Each class member basked in quiet fullness, feeling earth burdens dissolve. The power had built to a height so that our heavenly teachers from the Other Side could enter and be received into the room. They were four in number, named Apollo, Orion, Dyanthesis and Wake Robin. You could always tell when the guides entered, as there was a marked difference in the atmosphere, and we all felt it.

As our two worlds impinged simultaneously, I now saw, in extended sight, color tones from the etheric dimension, as reality shifted into a higher octave and the energy increased thousandfold. Color swirled in the atmosphere, darting, circling, spiraling points of light, delicate photons and quickened quanta my earth eyes would fail to perceive under ordinary circumstances charged the room with the silvery blue lavender of tranquility, rosy peach of gratitude, soft seafoam green of awareness, delicate pink lavender of inspiration, and the smoky pinkish lavender-blue of humility. The white walls of evening turned mauve before my eyes, as colors flecked with golden spots danced in front of my vision, against the play of shadow on the surfaces of the room.

I was aware of tremendous energy the color of chartreuse around a seventy-year old man I would soon know was Glenn Dies, Mary's youngest brother, who would become one of my best friends in life, my great horseback riding companion, and like a second father to me. Another person I noticed was a stately, gently smiling woman with clear blue eyes, upswept dark hair and a beautiful mezzo soprano voice named Sylvia Howe. Sylvia was seated between her husband, Andrew, whom she had met in the classes, and a physicist named Frank, whose wife Ruth, who had also been in the teaching, had recently passed away. Frank was now living with the Howes in their three storied rambling Victorian home on Fair Oaks Boulevard.

We remained in the power for a few minutes, absorbing heightened energy that enabled us to realize well beyond what we would ordinarily be capable of. My anticipation grew. I had yet to meet Mary, though I'd heard so much about her and had built up an enormous curiosity and desire to see her and bask in her orbit.

At last!

What a momentous event. I shall never forget my first glimpse of Mary.

She was diminutive in stature, but large in being, snow white haired and porcelain-skinned, with twinkling brown eyes that at once reflected the lustrous innocence of a child, yet glowed with inspired thoughts of the ancient of days. There was something extraordinarily compassionate and at the same time mischievous about her. She gave the impression of entertaining a wonderful cosmic secret that was profound and humorous. She was radiant, encased in light, her all-embracing smile spreading a wide arc of wisdom and love. She wore a silken flowered dress in varying hues of her keynote colors of the spiritual Arc of Purple – beautiful shades of lavender, violet, orchid, lilac, purple, heliotrope, wisteria. A jeweled broach on her bodice shone faintly like a star on a rainy evening as a pale streak of fiery ruby rose flashed through it. I felt from the moment I saw Mary, she had the power to show me the unseen things of another world.

Upon Mary's unexpected entrance, the power that surrounded the group struck a heightened responsive chord, and the energy increased. The light in the room glistened softly on the sheen of Mary's dress, as she began speaking about life between two worlds, how our physical existence on earth and the invisible realms of Heaven are intricately interconnected, and how we are able to reach that world both every night in our sleep, and when we enter 4th dimensional consciousness at any time of day.

Living in eternity now, and it's one world without end, amen, she always reminded us, that and those who have left us are as close as our hands and feet. She would speak inspiringly, telling about the class's experiences in the temples that week, what she herself had been told by the teachers there and how it applied to us. She would relate homespun anecdotes about her family, her past and stories about others that related to the work. She would tell us stories from the Dead Sea Scrolls she had translated. As she spoke, she was down to earth, mirthful, unassuming, and at the once, very much of the earth yet seemingly a native of another sphere. Rapt attention focused on her from the class. It was not so much what she said as her mere presence that nurtured us. If she often reverted to the same themes, everything she said always sounded as if one were hearing it for the first time. The truth was, Mary Weddell could have read the telephone book and it would have been a moving moment of truth.

Each Plane has many temples, she repeated, and in each temple are examining rooms in which one's entire life is gone over before an august body of heavenly teachers. "You see yourself clearly through mirrors, see the mistakes you've been making and how you can change your life. You see those black mirrors that reveal your detriments and the clear mirrors where you see your positive credits. Gazing into octagonal mirrors enables you to realize life in terms of forces rather than form, and you're given deeper insight into cosmic law, especially an understanding of opposite poles. We're looking to overcome the traits that are holding us back. We deal with memory patterns buried in the subconscious – guilt, fear, anger, criticism, resentment, selfishness. All these qualities have to be faced and eliminated before we can progress.

"On the examining Planes," Mary said, "you wonder where did they get all this information? And you almost feel they're spying, they seem to know so much about you."

Class members reported their previous week's experiences at the Temple of Reality on the 5th Plane. Some were written accounts, some impromptu recollections dawning on the spot, encouraged by the developing power that surrounded us. Students related visions, insights, and healings from their nightwork. Amazingly, many descriptions matched, experiences coincided, gaps were filled in. Students described meeting the same heavenly teachers, having been given identical guidance, they brought back similar messages that fit together like a glove. Mary mentioned how earth states of consciousness are given healing on all the Planes, and that we're shown how we can avoid past mistakes. After we are given spiritual initiations by the higher guides from the Hierarchy of St. John, we return back to our bodies, as pictured on the left side of the chart we were presently referring to.

Mary would then take questions. Time sped by as if the two hours spent were but a few minutes. We would always close with the class singing "How Great Thou Art." Several voices stood out, especially Mary's powerful contralto and Sylvia Howe's full-bodied mezzo. I was struck by the beauty and the phrasing of their voices. The hymns our class sang were always thrilling, and the most thrilling of all was "How Great Thou Art."

The heavenly guides stayed with us till the end of the class, and you could always tell when they left, for the whole atmosphere of the class was immediately altered, subdued, as if an electrical current had been switched off.

After Friday class came Fellowship, in which refreshments were served in the big kitchen toward the back of the house. There was always a selection of juices, coffee, tea, crudités, sandwiches, fruit, cookies, cakes, pies and other fare, much of it prepared by Miriam, some of it brought by students.

Gradually, I would learn more about the "Pasadena people," as we sometimes referred to them. Four persons lived in the large house with its several extensions that belonged to Violet Stevens. In addition to Mary, Miriam and Violet, the other inhabitant was and a tall, lanky, gangly, bent over stringbean of a fellow in his early 90's with a booming baritone voice named Jack. Jack was a dedicated artist who had devoted a lifetime of study to the Kabala, whose paintings of the Tree of Life hung on one of the walls in the front studio. Jack's voice always soared from the back of the room, particularly when singing "How Great Thou Art," especially in the refrain: "Then sings my soul, my Savior God to thee!"

Violet Stevens was a onetime belle of the ball at debutante parties toward the turn of the 20th century, along with her twin sister Edith. The Bond sisters were contemporaries of President Theodore Roosevelt's daughter Alice. Violet was the author of *Into the Light*, a fascinating autobiographical account of her life from early Washington Square, New York days with her wealthy widowed businessman father and her twin, then later as the wife of the popular Los Angeles bishop, the Right Reverend W. Bertrand Stevens (1884-1947), and following that, her years with Mary Weddell.

Violet's late husband, onetime rector of St. Anne's Episcopal Church in the Bronx, New York, had become the youngest bishop in the United States, when at 35 he was elected to serve as Los Angeles's second bishop, to preside over the diocese, its bishopric and the cavernous St. Paul's Cathedral in downtown L.A. Bishop Stevens was a scholar and outdoorsman who had earned both Masters and Ph D degrees and was considered a very fine literary writer. Highly esteemed by his colleagues, a pioneer in women's rights and children's advocate, Bishop Stevens died at age 63 from complications due to surgery. "Bert" and Violet had four daughters, one of whom, Emily, like her father, became an Episcopal priest.

Violet's twin, Edith Lawrence, had recently passed over. One of Violet's four daughters was the mother of seven sons, all named for apostles - Matthew, Mark, Luke, John, James, Peter, Bartholomew and Thomas. A striking large painting by Miriam of Violet's daughter and her brood of boys, plus their spotted hound, covered one wall of Mary's living room.

Members of the generation-spanning Friday night group ranged from a 17 year old Tibetan Buddhist to a sprightly 95 year old literary agent, President of the local chapter of the Penwomen of America. Some of the students were married couples, three of whom had met in the classes, others were widowed or single. While the majority had been raised in Christian denominations – Catholic and various Protestant sects – some were Jewish, some Buddhists. Most were college graduates, several with masters degrees, a handful with Ph D's. They were engineers, physicists, psychologists, real estate brokers, accountants, teachers, social workers, small business owners, two religious ministers in local churches, one factory worker, two "old China hands" who had operated a business in pre-World War II Shanghai. One was a corporate executive who ran a division of a Fortune 500 company, heading up a staff of 300,000. This man had a company jet at his perpetual disposal, and sometimes invited others on weekend and holiday trips to San Francisco, London or other locations to attend spiritual seminars.

The class was artistically and musically inclined – three quarters of the group played piano, five were organists; we had two violinists, one cellist, assorted guitarists, one harpist, and one flautist (the aforesaid Miriam A); four or five (myself included) had trained as classical singers, and any number were amateur painters. A number of the group – Mary, Miriam, Violet, Jack, Glenn and others – had been born in the 19th century. Amazingly, all these older folks were razor-sharp, so alive, so interested in life, in each other and everything around them, with laser-like minds that never missed a trick. It was rare and wonderful to see elderly people with such zest for life. The "old timers" were a truly inspiring bunch, a testament to how rewarding an active mind can be in later years.

A group of cottages on the property in back of the house were inhabited by Mary's irrepressible, feisty sister Tasma Dies Carey and brother Glenn Dies; by Kathryn Wilson, the nonogenarian literary agent, and by eighty-something retired physician Dr. Puera Robeson and her companion, whose name escapes me. Two couples lived a stone's throw away the next block over: septugenarians-pushing-octogenarians Helen and Ed Von Gehr, the old China hands, whose home was full of priceless Chinese antiques acquired during their decades of living in pre-Revolutionary China; and Katie and John, a young couple who had met in the classes, fallen in love and were now the parents of an infant daughter, Mary Elizabeth, named for Mary Weddell. Katie's mother, Grace, was Friday night's chief organist (although four others, including Miriam Willis, Helen von Gehr, Margaret Branchflower, or Mary could pinch hit when necessary). A strikingly pretty, blue-eyed, dark-haired girl named Clara, Sylvia Howe's twenty-something niece, was married to Bill (another class romance). They had two toddlers.

I remember vividly so many class members still: George, Fred, Frank, Ed, two Bills, John, Gene, Andrew, Ralph, Jack, Glenn, Dale, Willard, Bernard, Richard, Robert, Michael, Carmen, Linda, Carol, Violet, Rowena, Barbara, Evelyn, Katie, Sylvia, Gertrude, Eva, Ellen, Margaret, two Esthers, Miriam A., Henrietta, Ruth, Connie, Mary Jean, Judith, Helen, Alma, Lorna, Shelley, Eleanor, Diane, Pat, Elizabeth, Virginia, Ann, Doris, Clara, Jane ... Just as Carmen and George had said, it was truly a special bond we enjoyed , a particular one I have never found anywhere else.

I embraced the teaching immediately, accepting it as second nature, completely natural in its embodying of truth, wisdom and love. I was in sympathy, a lifetime "true believer." Both in childhood and in adulthood, I'd had experiences of the oneness of our two worlds. I had never doubted; since my earliest years, this truth had always been a part of me. I remembered my birth, there was never a doubt where I had come from and where I would some day return. That there could be an intermediary, a channel from earth connecting the two worlds in such a meaningful way not only comforted me but challenged me as well. It was a reaffirmation that strengthened and reinforced my convictions and experience.

I was happy to learn that I was to be included in those Mary picked up and took out at night, and that soon, my deceased grandparents and great aunt would join us every night.

# Planes of the Heavenworld
## by Jeanne Rejaunier
## Chapter Three: Great Souls

Mary Weddell, née Mary Elizabeth Dies, born in California in 1886, was the oldest of six children whose parents adopted an additional six youngsters. The lively Dies family moved to the mid-west, where Mary grew up and where her father pursued his occupation of building houses, before eventually moving the brood back to California. Mary's entire family – brothers, sisters, and parents, were all deeply involved in Theosophy, and from an early age, Mary herself proved to be a natural clairvoyant and medium, gifts which, however, she always downplayed.

It was love at first sight when Mary met her soul mate, Dr. George Weddell, physician and pioneer cancer researcher who had developed a skin cancer salve, the formula which he donated to humanity. The couple shared a rare affinity of mind and spirit. Both were devoted students of ancient wisdom; both were clairvoyant and saw etheric colors.

While still in her twenties, Mary was afflicted with infected tonsils, followed by bouts of pneumonia and tuberculosis, all of which left her debilitated and bedridden. One morning she woke paralyzed and unable to walk. Doctors who examined her, including the Mayo brothers, believed the infected tonsils had poisoned her system, and gave little hope for recovery, saying it was doubtful Mary would ever walk again.

During this period, Mary devoted herself to learning ancient languages. As an opera student, she had already studied modern languages, and in school, Latin and Greek. Now she learned Sanskrit, Aramaic, Hebrew and other ancient tongues.

One day, waking from a nap after dreaming she could walk, Mary was startled to find she had indeed walked in her sleep, and was standing by a window. The pattern continued: dreaming of walking, waking having walked. Upon waking, she would see colors swirling around her. In prayer she asked for the meanings of the colors to be revealed, and thus, over a two year period, Mary's color teachings saw the light of day. The color system Mary received in inspiration totaled more than100 basic rays, including both psychological and spiritual colors and extended rays, each with its separate meaning and power.

Since Mary saw the colors in forms of a feather, she called the color combinations "fans," "arcs," and "plumes."

While doctors considered her cure a miracle, Mary knew the real miracle was the power of color. Would color work on others as well? In order to find out, the next step was to test, seeking proof by using color over a period of time in a series of cases. Jointly, Mary and Dr. George applied color to the patients in the doctor's practice. Whether in person or clairvoyantly from a distance, Mary would perceive a person's aura and fill in missing colors to complete the picture of health and well being. Knowing that if a patient's fear could be overcome prior to a surgical procedure, a good measure of success could be predicted, Dr. George would seclude himself in a room before surgery and use color on the patient to counteract fear, creating bridges to a positive emotion. At the same time he was executing this action he was also establishing a rapport with his patient on a subliminal level.

These experiments took place over a period of 20 years, during which time the couple discovered that color did indeed heal others physically, mentally, emotionally and spiritually. Assured thorough practical experience of color's efficacy, the Weddells began teaching. Their work met with great success in the US, England and France. Many years before the proclamation of the "Age of Aquarius" or "New Age," prior to World War II, Mary was teaching color in Los Angeles. Her first class consisted of 100 doctors and dentists. In time, she had a group of students from England and France who came to Southern California every other year to absorb her teachings.

Shortly after the end of World War II, Dr. George died suddenly from a heart attack after an auto accident in which he had stopped to administer to a victim. Around this same time, Mary was chosen to be one of the translators of the Dead Sea Scrolls, which gave her a unique insight into the Essene Teacher of Righteousness, said to be Jesus, who studied at the Temple of Heliopolis. Over ensuing years, Mary formulated her remarkable Planes of the Heavenworld course.

Miriam Barr Willis, artist, sculptress, painter, former surgical nurse and Episcopal nun, administrator and teacher who became Mary's invaluable assistant, was the youngest of eight children. Miriam grew up first in Ontario, Canada, then in prairie country in Alberta, in years full of droughts, blizzards and fire. A fall from her horse at age 15 left Miriam with a serious spinal injury, and like Mary, she too became paralyzed for a time. While she was still unable to walk, a prairie fire broke out and was heading straight for the Willis house, which had been built by Miriam's father and brothers. Hobbling on a pair of crutches fashioned by one of her brothers, Miriam prayed alongside her mother, while her father and brothers fought the fire. At the last moment, the winds shifted and the house was spared. Miriam was sent to a hospital 70 miles away to at last have her horse riding injury tended to. As she lay alone gazing at a star outside her window, it was as if the star spoke to her and told her she would recover and then devote her life to missionary work.

As a young woman, Miriam met fell in love with a man who was her soul mate, who sadly met a tragic premature death. It was an ideal love to which Miriam remained forever dedicated, and she kept her fiancé's picture in a locket next to her heart for the rest of her life. Soon after his death, Miriam became an Episcopal nun, a vocation she would pursue over the course of the next two dozen years as a teacher and surgical nurse.

In time, Miriam found the orthodox Church of England failed to answer many of her questions in the areas of higher consciousness and regarding the many visions of life after death she was experiencing. Advised in no uncertain terms by the convent's Mother Superior that her visions would have to stop, Miriam requested an audience with the bishop.

The bishop in turn assured her that yes, indeed, there was a life after life, and yes, many souls in the Afterlife do indeed communicate with those on the earth plane – it is, as Jesus said, one world without end, amen. However, the bishop said, religions were forced to downplay that aspect, since some people were afraid of it and in the modern era, it had become too sensitive and controversial an issue accepted by only a few, even though it had been a part of the original church's teachings. The contemporary Church of England could provide no comfort to Miriam's questions. Only outside the cloistered existence, upon meeting Mary Weddell, with the means of expanded consciousness revealed to her through color and the Planes, did Miriam find what she'd been seeking all her life. Not long after, Miriam Willis came to study with Mary, and after an apprenticeship in color, became Mary's assistant.

Miriam came to live with Mary's family and nursed Mary's mother in her final years. She later took a job at a pottery company, became a designer of ceramic flowers, and was also a quality control inspector for the local fire department. Later she went into business for herself, creating figurines of flowers and birds. Her work was exhibited at many art trade shows and sold to top department stores across the country. When Miriam came to live in the Pasadena house, she was given a building in back as her ceramics studio, where she turned to creating religious statues, many of which now graced the Pasadena home – Jesus, the Virgin, St. Francis and others.

Miriam was clairaudient and received additional material as she worked side by side with Mary to illustrate Mary's colors and Planes courses. Miriam always said that the knowledge of long-lost color meanings revealed to Mary and her development in the skill of using color were harmonious with what Jesus taught the disciples when he took them apart and taught them many things.

# Planes of the Heavenworld
## by Jeanne Rejaunier
## Chapter Sixteen - The Animal Kingdom

Linda asked, "What about pets? Are there animals such as dogs and cats on the Other Side? Where do our precious animal companions go when they pass?"

Mary said, "In Children's Land, I have seen lambs. I've not seen dogs or cats on the Other Side, although I've been told they are there. But I have seen the little lambs playing over the green and I've seen lots of birds there as well. I believe there is an Animal Kingdom, and I believe animals evolve. I have never been to the Animal Kingdom. but I have heard it exists. That is what I understand from what I've been told."

"I'm sure it exists, too," Mary Jean said. "It would absolutely, definitely have to exist. In fact, I read about the Animal Kingdom in a book by a medium who channeled information on the subject. And there are animal psychics around who communicate with discarnate animals, who say our pets go to the Heavenworld, just like we do."

Dale said, "Anyone who's ever lost a pet when the pet was being cared for at a veterinarian usually receives a very sweet card from the staff, all about how your pet has gone to Dog Heaven or Cat Heaven and is safe there, and that one day you and your animal will be reunited."

Mary said, "My husband and I were at Violet's sister Edith Lawrence's house for dinner one night. There was a great fireplace in the living room. After dinner, we were all preparing to sit around the fire. My chair was close to the fireplace but Edith's dog was so close to my chair I couldn't get into it. So I went around the Other Side of the chair and pushed past the dog. He was so close to my feet I could feel his warmth. He would hang his head away from the fire – I noticed he had very big head and a loose mouth.

"Every once in a while Edith would wonder, Mary what are you looking at? I asked Edith if she had ever had a big dog. Edith said yes, she had. I asked my husband, 'George, what do you see in front of the fireplace by my chair? Do you see that St. Bernard?'

"George asked, 'Edith, did you ever have a St. Bernard?'

"Edith said yes, I'll get you some pictures. She was very proud of the pictures she'd taken of this dog. He was a talented animal who did all kinds of wonderful things – sitting up, shaking hands, begging for doggie biscuits, carrying things, fetching the daily newspaper from the front porch, and so forth. The next thing I saw was the silliest little dog named Gippy. He'd only been gone a year or so. These two dogs used to play together. Edith said the little dog used to ride around on the back of the St. Bernard till the St. Bernard got so tired he'd shake the little dog off. The St. Bernard preceded little Gippy over to the Other Side. I had known Gippy but not the St. Bernard. I told Edith, 'Your big dog was so close to my chair it made me uncomfortable.'

"She said, 'He always used to lie there that way when I was alone.'"

Violet said, "Mary, one of the first times you came to the house before I had the alterations on it done, the back steps were different. You asked me, Violet, did you have a cat? A rosy peach colored cat? I said yes, indeed I did have, and we named that cat Georgia Peach, by the way. Mary told me, 'Your Georgia Peach is lying on the steps outside.'"

Mary said, "The cat was so real I tried to touch it. The cat must have been there for quite a while."

Violet said, "We chose Georgia Peach from the pound mainly because of her beautiful color. She turned into a splendid cat. It was only later, when I came to study color with Mary, that I learned why her pale rosy peach color appealed to me so much - it was because this is the color of gratitude."

"Class, where do we find the color of gratitude?" Mary asked.

"In the Spiritual Arc of Purple," Esther Barnes replied, "Gratitude is the 9th Ray of Purple. And from the meaning of this ray, gratitude is more than thankfulness or appreciation. Gratitude is rich, heartfelt, overflowing appreciation."

Violet said, "And you know, as much as animals can express human emotions, I believe Georgia Peach felt enormous gratitude for our having taken her out of the pound, adopting her and giving her a loving home those years we had her. She was a lovely cat."

Mary smiled and said, "That's all I can tell you about animals."

Pat said, "To relate to your story of seeing the St. Bernard and the little dog Gippy, Mary, I'm sure, absolutely convinced beyond a shadow of a doubt that our pets return to us in spiritual visitations. Especially if they loved their homes, and if they are at a high level in their animal evolvement, they return to their homes after they pass. I say this because I've had the experience. My deceased pets have returned to visit us on several occasions. Even my husband was aware of it."

Barbara said, "Our family has had the same experience. Willard and Jennifer will confirm it. Whenever our cat visits us from the Other Side, we hear a knocking inside a certain piece of furniture – it's always Willard's desk in the den. You can't miss it. And you immediately know what it is."

Willard said, "I can confirm this, Mary."

Evelyn said. "I've had that same experience. And an interesting phenomenon in my case – our new pet, Alex, who replaced Mimi, our pet who recently died, is aware of and can see Mimi's spirit. This usually happens at night. It's very obvious to us."

Virginia said, "I've heard it's commonplace for animals to sense discarnate spirits. Animals are so sensitive and intuitive, they have very strong ESP, they're connected and tuned in to spirit in ways that we humans are not."

"Cats are always aware of departed animal spirits," Helen agreed. "Maybe this is one reason the Egyptians valued and revered cats so much – for their knowledge of and connection to the Afterlife."

"I had this experience: our new cat, Sam, is very visibly aware when our deceased cat, Cali, comes back to visit us," Rowena said. "You can always tell by Sam's reactions when Cali is in the room. The particular way Sam goes into alert, holds his head at attention, pricks up his ears, holds his body in one position, motionless, can't take his eyes off a certain spot, and seems almost to be in a trance, communicating with our kitty from the Other Side – these are signs that occur each and every time."

Glenn said, "Mary, I've seen horses on the Other Side, and just about every horse I ever owned has come to me after they passed. They nuzzle me to let me know they're all right. I can even hear them nicker softly. They'll lip me and breathe into my ear. When a horse puts his head close to yours and breathes into your ear, that's a sign of true love. There's a lot of my horses on the Other Side who've come back and done that."

"Glenn was always a great horse lover," Mary told the class, smiling at her younger brother, "from the time he was a little boy. He's owned many horses in the different parts of the country he's lived in."

"You hate to lose your horse," Glenn said, "because a horse is such a true friend, a friend like no other. But then, after he leaves this earth world and that horse comes back to visit you, he's telling you not to worry about him. And you see he's really got it made over there on the Other Side, so you do feel a lot better about losing him."

"I think we can all feel better about the separation from our loved ones, not just our animals, but our human loved ones," Margaret said, "knowing what we know about the Planes in the Heavenworld."

########

## ALSO BY JEANNE REJAUNIER

**Fiction**

The Beauty Trap
The Motion and the Act
Affair in Rome
Mob Sisters
Odalisque at the Spa

**Nonfiction**

Planes of the Heavenworld
My Sundays with Henry Miller
Modeling From the Ground Up
The 50 Best Careers in Modeling

All books are available in print and on all eBook platforms - for computer, tablet, eReader and smart phone

## CRITICS' REVIEWS

## THE BEAUTY TRAP, by JEANNE REJAUNIER

"Here is a novel that can't miss, crammed with all the ingredients that make a blockbuster." - **Publishers Weekly**

"A startling closeup of the world's most glamorous business, an intensely human story." - **The New York Times**

"Jeanne Rejaunier has concocted a sexpourri of life among the mannequins that's spiked with all the ingredients of a blockbuster bestseller."- **Playboy**

"A fascinating inside story of the most glamorous girls in the business, absorbing to read." - **California Stylist**

"A powerful novel that takes off like 47 howitzers." - **San Fernando Valley (CA) Magazine**

"New York's most sought after women find themselves having to make desperate decisions that will affect their very lives." - **Wilmington (DE) News Journal**.

"The novel is rich in esoteric commercial lore about modeling...." **Saturday Review**

"Possibly the most honest novel to appear by a female writer in the past decade."- **Literary Times**

"Crammed with all the ingredients of a blockbuster. ..Beasts in the Beauty Jungle... authentic, searing exposé." **London Evening News**

"Miss Rejaunier is most interesting when she goes behind the scenes in the modeling world." - **Detroit Free Press**

"If a male author had written *The Beauty Trap*, he'd be hanged by the thumbs." - **UPI**

# COMING SOON FROM JEANNE REJAUNIER (2015-2016)

## Fiction

All That Glitters
The Zoetron Revelation
Secrets of an Odalisque

## Nonfiction

Hollywood Sauna
Where Did the Money Go?
Astrology For Lovers (2015 updated edition)

#########

## CONNECT WITH AUTHOR
## JEANNE REJAUNIER ONLINE

Nearly 200 of Jeanne's videos can be seen on YouTube:
http://www.youtube.com/user/jrej?feature=mhee.

Worldwide publicity from Jeanne's books, including her bestselling novel about the modeling business, *The Beauty Trap; The Motion and the Act,* about California New Agers in search of perfect sex; *Affair in Rome,* and several of her nonfiction titles can be viewed at:
http://www.youtube.com/watch?v=PyxXbu24s04&list=UUEq7ATRVTR8sfBbQmBk3w3Q&index=14&feature=plcp:

and at:
http://www.youtube.com/watch?v=N9NCObTQArU&list=UUEq7ATRVTR8sfBbQmBk3w3Q&index=17&feature=plcp

Additional Rejaunier writing is found on Jeanne's blog:
http://www.jarcollect.blogspot.com.

Connect with Jeanne on Facebook:
http://www.facebook.com/profile.php?id=1171012552

and at: http://www.facebook.com/BooksByJeanneRejaunier

Connect with Jeanne on Google +:
https://plus.google.com/u/0/photos/104645427544174014108/albums

Connect with Jeanne on Amazon Author Central:
http://www.amazon.com/-/e/B001K7XL12

#####

JEANNE REJAUNIER

Manufactured by Amazon.ca
Bolton, ON